David's Faith

*A 30-Day Women's Devotional Based on
the Life of King David*
Mary Jane Humes

David's Faith: A 30 Day Women's Devotional Based on the Life of King David

Faith Series Devotionals, Volume 1

Mary Jane Humes

Published by Mary Jane Humes, 2021.

While every precaution has been taken in the preparation of this book, the publisher assumes no responsibility for errors or omissions, or for damages resulting from the use of the information contained herein.

DAVID'S FAITH: A 30 DAY WOMEN'S DEVOTIONAL BASED ON THE LIFE OF KING DAVID

First edition. June 21, 2021.

Copyright © 2021 Mary Jane Humes.

ISBN: 978-1736038932

Written by Mary Jane Humes.

This book is lovingly dedicated to the precious memory of my mother—Dorothy M. Rhodes. Every evening she would gather the family together to read to us from a children's devotional, a Bible commentary, and also a chapter of the Bible. It was because of this practice that at the age of four, I told her I wanted to get saved. She then led me to the Lord. During the time I was writing this book, she encouraged me and prayed for me and desired to finally be able to read it. However, the God of David, whom she loved and faithfully served, had other plans for her; He called her to be with Him on January 6, 2018. While I miss her very much, to be with Christ is far better than any experience on earth. I am so thankful to her for all of her love, prayers, and best wishes for me, as well as her consistent Christian testimony.

Copyright © 2020 by Mary Jane Humes.

All rights reserved. No part of this publication may be reproduced, distributed, or transmitted in any form or by any means, including photocopying, recording, or other electronic or mechanical methods, without the prior written permission of the publisher, except in the case of brief quotations embodied in critical reviews and certain other noncommercial uses permitted by copyright law. For permission requests, write to the author at hello@maryjanehumes.com.

All Scripture quotations, unless otherwise indicated, are from the Authorized (King James) Version. Rights in the Authorized Version in the United Kingdom are vested in the Crown. Reproduced by permission of the Crown's patentee, Cambridge University Press.

Proofreading and typesetting: Sally Hanan of Inksnatcher.com

Cover design: Reba Covers[1]

Ordering Information: Quantity sales. Special discounts are available on quantity purchases by corporations, associations, and others. For details, contact the author at hello@maryjanehumes.com.

David's Faith: A 30-Day Women's Devotional Based on the Life of King David/ Mary Jane Humes

ISBN Print: 9781736038932

eBook ISBN: 978-1-7360389-2-5

---

1. http://www.fiverr.com/rebecacovers/design-professional-book-cover-or-ebook-cover

This book is lovingly dedicated to the precious memory of my mother—Dorothy M. Rhodes. Every evening she would gather the family together to read to us from a children's devotional, a Bible commentary, and also a chapter of the Bible. It was because of this practice that at the age of four, I told her I wanted to get saved. She then led me to the Lord. During the time I was writing this book, she encouraged me and prayed for me and desired to finally be able to read it. However, the God of David, whom she loved and faithfully served, had other plans for her; He called her to be with Him on January 6, 2018. While I miss her very much, to be with Christ is far better than any experience on earth. I am so thankful to her for all of her love, prayers, and best wishes for me, as well as her consistent Christian testimony.

Contents

Introduction

1. David—A Man after God's Own Heart
2. "I Have Seen..."
3. David and Goliath, Part 1
4. David and Goliath, Part 2—Give God the Glory
5. David Behaves Himself Wisely
6. David Flees to Samuel
7. Jonathan Protects David
8. David Gets Goliath's Sword
9. David Cares for His Parents
10. Massacre of Faithful Priests
11. David Delivers Keilah from the Philistines
12. David and Jonathan in the Wilderness of Ziph
13. David Spares Saul in Engedi
14. Abigail Captures David's Heart
15. David Spares Saul's Life Again
16. Send David Home
17. David Recovers All
18. Israel's Civil War
19. The Death of Ishbosheth
20. David's Third and Final Anointing as King
21. David Does a Good Thing the Right Way
22. When God Says No
23. David and Mephibosheth
24. David's Affair with Bathsheba
25. The Fallout of David's Affair
26. Absalom's Revolt
27. Deal Gently with Absalom
28. David's Mighty Men ... Except for Joab
29. David Numbers the People
30. David's Inheritance to Solomon

31. David's Death and the Aftermath

Dear Friend

Glossary

Acknowledgments
About the Author
Can You Help?

Introduction

In my many years of going to church, learning, and listening, I thought I had an average grasp of the basics of the Bible. Perhaps I did, since I grew up in a Christian home, went to a Christian school, and went to Sunday school. However, as an adult, I talked to several women who did not have a good, if any, understanding of some of the stories of the great heroes of the Bible, especially those in the Old Testament, David being one of them. Those who did know something about ancient history as recorded in the Bible did not realize these taught biblical "stories" were also for us today. Even though some may read their Bibles daily, people read without comprehension too often, so I felt that some teaching about these Bible characters would be beneficial.

I once taught a Sunday school class on the life of David; and the memories of what I studied to teach my class, and attempted to make alive for my students, became the basis of this book. During the time I was teaching the Sunday school class, one lady at church remarked, "Everyone loves David!"

The character of David is so attractive because we can all relate to him, and he is one of the Bible's best heroes. He is a man who went from poverty to riches and experienced both failures and successes. And though he was neither an exemplary husband nor father, he was still a powerful warrior who protected his nation and never lost a battle. He wrote most of the book of Psalms, and he is referred to as the "sweet psalmist of Israel." Ironically, David battled with bouts of depression and fear, which is conveyed poignantly in many of his psalms, including his most famous one of all, Psalm 23. Despite his failures, David is referred to by God as "a man after mine own heart" (Acts 13:22).

This book is a devotional based on events in the life of David, the second king of Israel, who is referred to as a man after God's own heart (1Samuel 13:14). Daily, for a thirty-day period, there is:

- a Bible reading about one of the events in David's life and one of his psalms,
- a Bible lesson that recaps that particular incident in his life,
- a section called Ponderings of a Woman after God's Own Heart,
- what we can learn from David, and
- a suggested prayer.

The King David story is recorded in the biblical books of Samuel, Kings, and Chronicles. After studying the thirty events in the life of David highlighted in this book, I hope you will go back and read the full account of David's life as recorded in the Bible.

David went from being an unknown shepherd boy to the greatest king Israel ever knew. He was a direct ancestor of Christ, and he was promised by God that his throne would be established by Him forever (2 Samuel 7:16). This promise and prophecy of God is referring to the millennial reign of Jesus Christ (the most famous Son of David) after His second coming.

It is my desire that you will learn more about David while challenging your own Christian life in order to become more of a woman after God's own heart. My hope and prayer for you is that this little book will help you to draw closer to the God of David.

In Christ,
Mary Jane Humes

Author's Note

Many times in Scripture, and sometimes in my writing, the word "Lord" is used when referring to a particular passage of Scripture. This designation with all capital letters is not a typo, nor is it used to show importance. Many times the name of God, referred to as Lord, is the translation of *Jehovah* in the Old Testament.

The reason for all capitals versus the capital "L" followed by lowercase letters is to differentiate the meanings between two different Hebrew words, both translated into the English language as "Lord." The word translated into the English language from the Hebrew is Lord, all capitals, denoting God's personal name. The word "Lord" (as compared to Lord) is one of His titles. Psalm 8:1 "O Lord our Lord..." is an excellent example, showing the reader there are different meanings for the same word. The word "Lord" (Jehovah) is not a title of God, it is rather a name of God, specifically God's personal name.

When the Bible uses the name Lord, the writer is implying a closeness, a friendship, between God and the speaker. It is saying the mighty Creator God and the speaker are on a first-name basis. It is similar to calling your friend by her first name rather than the more formal but very accurate title of Mrs. Jones, for example. When you see the name of God as Lord —all capital letters, know God is showing us that He and the one using His name have a close, friendly, trusting relationship. Many Bible scholars, and I, too, believe the names of both Jehovah and Lord refer to the second Person of the Godhead, none other than the preincarnate Jesus Christ.

– –

Day 1
David—A Man after God's Own Heart

Daily Bible Reading: 1 Samuel 16:1–13 and Psalm 8

Today's Verse: "The Lord said unto Samuel, Look not on his countenance, or on the height of his stature; because I have refused him: for the Lord seeth not as man seeth; for man looketh on the outward appearance, but the Lord looketh on the heart." (1 Samuel 16:7)

Bible Lesson: This is the chapter in which we are introduced to David. God sent the prophet Samuel to the family of Jesse to find the next king. God told Samuel He was going to take the kingdom of Israel away from King Saul and give it to a man after His own heart (Acts 13:22). Samuel's job was to find the future king and anoint him.

Jesse had eight sons. Samuel started with the oldest of Jesse's sons, Eliab, who presented himself before Samuel. He was tall, good-looking, and no doubt had a kingly bearing. Samuel thought, *This must be the one,* but God said, "No, I have refused him: for the Lord ... looketh on the heart" (v. 7). This same scenario was repeated six more times, with Samuel inspecting each of the young men. After the last one was rejected, Samuel must have thought either God made a mistake or there was another son who had not been brought before him.

Out of desperation, Samuel asked Jesse the obvious question, "Are here all thy children?" (v. 11). Jesse admitted his youngest was keeping the sheep. Obviously, Jesse considered the youngest member of his family as not important enough, or just plain too young; but Samuel said, "Send and fetch him: for we will not sit down till he come hither" (v. 11). Samuel was probably thinking something to the effect of, *This has to be the one; there's no one else left.*

DAVID'S FAITH: A 30 DAY WOMEN'S DEVOTIONAL BASED ON THE LIFE OF KING DAVID

God confirmed to Samuel that this young man, the eighth son of Jesse—David by name—was the one chosen by Him to be the future king of Israel. He was, we find out, the man after God's own heart.

At this first meeting of David, an understanding of David's heart is not obvious. However, as we study the life, actions, and words of David contained in Psalms, the focus of his heart becomes quite evident. As he matured in years and experiences, he never stopped trusting in God, even in times of extreme personal grief and disappointment.

Ponderings of a Woman after God's Heart: David was the eighth son of Jesse. According to Bible scholars, the number eight in the Bible is the number of new beginnings. David was the start of a new line of kings in Israel, a line of kings God promised would continue "forever" (2 Samuel 7:16). This promise God gave David was a forward look to the millennial reign of Jesus Christ, the Son of David, at his second advent.

If you are reading this devotional, you obviously desire to learn how to be a woman after God's own heart. Once you have accepted the free gift of God's great salvation through Jesus Christ (Romans 6:23; 10:9–10), you are commanded to "grow in grace and in the knowledge of our Lord and Savior Jesus Christ" (2 Peter 3:18).

Here are the three basics of becoming a woman after God's own heart:

1. *Daily prayer* – This devotional has suggested prayers based on each daily topic; however, use these only as a tiny supplement to your prayer life. Learn to develop a daily prayer time when you can communicate all the desires of your heart to God.
2. *Daily Bible reading* – If you have not yet cultivated the habit of reading the Bible daily, this devotional is designed to help you. Each day there is a portion of Scripture concerning David and one of his psalms for you to read.
3. *Regular church attendance* – It is very important that you attend a church that faithfully teaches and preaches the Bible.

Regular fellowship with other Christians is not only important to your daily walk with God; it is commanded by Him: "Not forsaking the assembling of ourselves together, as the manner of some is; but exhorting one another" (Hebrews 10:25). Christians need to regularly fellowship with other Christians.

Thoughts on Psalm 8: This psalm may have been written by David as a very young man, a shepherd boy, before he was anointed king. Perhaps David wrote this particular psalm when he had to stay awake at night and watch the sheep. He may have been referring to himself when he said, "Out of the mouth of babes and sucklings hast thou ordained strength" (v. 2).

In this glorious psalm, David praised God because of His wonderful creation. David realized the vastness of God's power, and he marveled that God even thinks of mankind. David knew God gave man the responsibility to care for His beautiful creation. David also seemed to know something about the angelic realm, because he said God made man a little lower than the angels (v. 5).

If this psalm was written by David at a very young age, it shows David truly had a heart for God and for the things of God. The next time you take in the beauty of nature, I encourage you to remember this psalm and to praise God for His wonderful creation.

Prayer

Dear heavenly Father, I thank You that You look on the heart and not my appearance. Help me to have a heart for You that I may live my life pleasing to You in all my ways. When I sin against You, help me to quickly come to You to confess my sin, knowing You will forgive me. Help me to serve You by regularly praying, reading Your Word, and attending Your house of worship. In Christ's name, amen.

— —

Day 2
"I Have Seen..."

Daily Bible Reading: 1 Samuel 16:14–23 and Psalm 1

Today's Verse: "Then answered one of the servants, and said, Behold, I have seen a son of Jesse the Bethlehemite, that is cunning in playing, and a mighty valiant man, and a man of war, and prudent in matters, and a comely person, and the Lord is with him." (1 Samuel 16:18)

Bible Lesson: Back in Old Testament times, God's spirit was not sealed in His people as He is in the present age of grace. Saul was in a downward spiral. He knew he would never leave the legacy of his kingdom to any of his sons. In fact, he knew his days as king were numbered. Today's scripture tells us God's spirit had departed from Saul and that an evil spirit was sent by God to trouble him.

These were dark days for Saul, and for his servants also, because they could never be sure of their king's mood, but they had a good suggestion. They believed that if someone played peaceful, soothing music with a harp for Saul, it would help him. One of them suggested David, saying, "I have seen a son of Jesse the Bethlehemite, that is cunning in playing" (1 Samuel 16:18).

The servant went on to describe David—he played well, was a valiant man of war, prudent in matters, a good-looking person (the word in the Bible is "comely"), and most importantly of all, "The Lord is with him" (v. 18). This kind of person was exactly what Saul's servants needed to help their master—the comforting, steadying influence of the Lord through someone indwelt by Him.

Ponderings of a Woman after God's Heart: The phrase "I have seen" is interesting. The servants of Saul were observing David. Even though they did not seem to know his name (they referred to him as "a son of Jesse"), David's reputation preceded him. But most importantly for this royal job, they saw he was both "prudent in matters" and "the Lord is with him."

David may or may not have realized he was under such scrutiny. Like David, you, too, are being watched. People see you. Good or bad, your life is an open book.

Do you desire to be "prudent in matters" also? The word "prudent" means to be careful or wise in handling practical matters, to exercise good judgment or common sense. Being prudent or wise in your everyday activities is a good testimony to showing you are a Christian and also to showing that making good decisions is always beneficial, in every way.

Each day comes with its own assortment of practical matters composed of decisions, choices, relationships, and trials; and these matters occur in all areas of our lives—family, jobs, church, friends, etc. It is a monumental challenge to be prudent in all of these matters.

Each one of us needs both help and wisdom on a daily basis. Thankfully, there is a promise from God that He will give us wisdom—His wisdom. James 1:5 reads, "If any of you lack wisdom, let him ask of God, that giveth to all men liberally, and upbraideth not; and it shall be given him." This is such a beautiful promise!

David was prudent in matters because God was with him. He must have asked God for wisdom, and, of course, God gave it to him. It is a good practice to pray throughout the day for wisdom from God to guide you with your many daily tasks. Those who are watching you will see you, too, are "prudent in matters."

Thoughts on Psalm 1: This psalm introduces the entire book of Psalms, contrasting the godly with the ungodly. The psalm starts with the word "blessed," which may be interpreted as "happy." The psalmist went on to tell how a person can achieve happiness.

The first verse is negative, telling those who would be happy to shun all the ways of the ungodly, the sinners, and the scornful. The next verse is positive: to find happiness, you are to delight in the law of the Lord.

The godly ones are compared to a planted, fruitful tree; they will prosper like a tree bearing fruit year after year. The Lord knows these people, those who love His law, and He will protect and keep them.

Verse 5 is interesting and shows David was a prophet when he said, "Therefore the ungodly shall not stand in the judgment." This is quite possibly a reference to a bodily and glorious resurrection and the judgment of God. While judgment usually carries a bad connotation, this one does not. At this resurrection and judgment, God will usher the godly into heaven, judging their works and rewarding them accordingly. Entering heaven and appearing before the God of all creation is a privilege reserved only for godly people.

The ungodly do not have this hope since, according to David, they will not even appear there. The ungodly, though they may appear to prosper in this life, will disappear. They are like chaff, the husks of the wheat grain, that will blow away with the wind. Their ways and deeds will perish, unlike those of the righteous, who will flourish for eternity.

Prayer

Dear heavenly Father, please give me the wisdom today and every day to be wise in all of my decisions. Help me to be prudent in all of my matters, and give me the strength to do what is right before You and others. I know I am being observed. Help me to be a good example of a godly Christian woman to all those watching me. I need Your wisdom to live my everyday life so others will see You in me. Thank You for Your promises. I pray in the name of the Savior. Amen.

— —

Day 3
David and Goliath, Part 1

Daily Bible Reading: 1 Samuel 17:1–32 and Psalm 37

Today's Verse: "The Philistine drew near morning and evening and presented himself forty days." (1 Samuel 17:16)

Bible Lesson: The whole chapter of 1 Samuel 17 is about David and Goliath. Even though this is a popular Bible story for children, there is encouragement found in this passage for the Christian woman who is feeling beaten down and discouraged.

Goliath was a real giant. This, and everything else recorded in the Bible, is not merely a story but a true account of history. Bible scholars generally agree Goliath was between nine and ten feet tall, and his armor weighed about 156 pounds. For forty days, Goliath's boastful speech was gradually undermining and weakening the morale of the Israelites. The number forty in the Bible represents a time of testing and trial.

David got to the camp of the Israelites early in the morning, and he was chatting with his brothers when he heard the giant's challenge and saw his brothers' fear. Even after forty days, the terror of both the man and his message was still fresh. The promise of great rewards for killing the giant included not only a lot of money but also an invitation into the royal family through marriage to one of the princesses. And if that was not enough, the whole family would be tax exempt. This magnanimous reward was something coveted by all, yet it seemed unattainable. The giant appeared impossible to kill. Aside from his size, he was also very heavily armed. Defeat Goliath and you'd defeat the entire Philistine army.

For all of the forty days, the Israelite soldiers proposed plans, considered them, and rejected them. During this time, they must have prayed for God to help. Maybe they wanted God to send a heavenly army of armed angels to wipe out Goliath and the entire Philistine army, but for forty days there was no help in sight. The only viable plan, it seemed, was to wait until this guy died of old age.

God allowed forty days to go by before David appeared on the scene. Humbly and calmly, David said to King Saul, "Let no man's heart fail because of him; thy servant will go and fight with this Philistine" (1 Samuel 17:32). His statement implied that not only was he going to fight, he was also going to kill the giant.

Ponderings of a Woman after God's Heart: We read this story and think, *Why didn't David get there sooner? Like maybe thirty-nine days earlier?*

You may feel like the Israelite army. You pray but you are still taunted morning and night with negative and distressing thoughts. Your entire life seems like a war of attrition. Day after day you are being worn down by the cares of this world, which could include one or more of the following: financial distress, difficult family relationships health problems, or some other issue; there seems to be no help in sight. All you have is the promise of heaven after you die, and you sometimes wish for that day of death and heaven to come sooner rather than later!

The army of the Israelites called on God to help them, and help came in the form of David, but not until after thirty-nine long and tiring days had passed.

Let me kindly encourage you today to call out to God for help. He will send exactly what you need; however, it probably will not be in the form you will immediately understand nor in the time you want it to happen. I am sure the army of Israel did not see the answer to their prayers in David the youth, yet he was the one who solved their problem by killing the Philistine bully.

Remember, God cares for you. 1 Peter 5:7 gives us both a command and a promise: "Casting all your care upon him; for he careth for you." If you say God does not care about you, you are calling Him a liar.

In the psalm for today, David, the instrument God used to send deliverance from the Philistine giant, was the one who needed God's help in his life. He cried out to God to help him because he knew only God could intervene and help. Like David the psalmist, you should trust in God, cry out to Him, and wait for His deliverance.

Thoughts on Psalm 37: This is such an encouraging psalm. Written by David, possibly after he was king for a time, it contains the reflections, wisdom, and echoes of the experiences of one who had walked with his God for many years.

This portion of Scripture is full of compassion for those who are stressed and in distress, especially because of evildoers. David knew how difficult it was to wait on the Lord; yet he gently but firmly reminded us that as believers, we are known and cared for by God, although His timing is not our timing.

This hymn is full of wonderful promises for us to claim when we are feeling impatient and unable to succeed. The uplifting words in this psalm command us to keep doing what is right because God does see, He does care, and He will reward us. If you are going through some trial now but trusting in your Savior, you are doing what you are supposed to do. Let me join with David in encouraging you to trust in God more and to wait on Him for the wonderful blessings we cannot imagine.

Prayer

Dear heavenly Father, I need the help that can only come from You. There is none other to deliver me. I am tired, and I have exhausted my strength. Please give me some of Yours. Help me to trust You while I am waiting. Help me to glorify You even through my daily frustrations and trials. Thank You for caring for me and for the help You are sending even now. I pray this in the Messiah's name. Amen.

– –

Day 4
David and Goliath, Part 2—Give God the Glory

Daily Bible Reading: 1 Samuel 17:32–58 and Psalm 108

Today's Verse: "All this assembly shall know that the Lord saveth not with sword and spear: for the battle is the Lord 's, and he will give you into our hands." (1 Samuel 17:47)

Bible Lesson: Saul sent for David when he heard David had volunteered to kill the giant. However, Saul had his reservations about David's ability, since David was "but a youth" (1 Samuel 17:33), and Goliath had the experience of years of war. When David told Saul how he had killed both a lion and a bear that attacked his lambs, Saul knew David not only had experience, more importantly, the Lord would help David.

Unprotected with armor, and with only a sling for a weapon, David chose five stones—not because he thought he would miss the first time, but in case Goliath's four brothers showed up. Goliath's was one of five children (2 Samuel 21:16–22). David was prepared to kill the giant's brothers also.

In a practiced, skillful movement, David flung one of his five stones at Goliath's head, causing the boastful giant to fall face down to the ground. It seems to me Goliath literally fell before God on his face. Goliath was knocked unconscious and David, using Goliath's own sword, then hacked off his head.

Ponderings of a Woman after God's Heart: This battle was not just between two warriors rather than between two supernatural forces. Upon seeing David, Goliath cursed him by his gods. David replied that the Lord —the God of Israel, the one, true, living God—would deliver Goliath into the hand of David that very day.

In talking to King Saul earlier, David gave the credit to the Lord Jehovah for his victories over the lion and the bear, either one of which could have easily killed both the lamb and David. Again when facing Goliath, David gave God the credit before his victory over the giant.

God used David to kill the giant and bring deliverance to the Israelite army. David was strong, practiced, and skilled, but he knew it was God who gave the victory. God always uses people. There are so many different instances in my life when God either gave me a blessing or a direct answer to prayer, but He always used a person. Here is one example: I was given a very ill cat to help nurse back to health. The poor little guy was injured and left to die before he was rescued, vetted, and came to live with me. I knew he was recovering from his ordeal, so it did not alarm me that he was lethargic; however, one particular day he seemed worse. That evening he disappeared, and I found him in a dark corner of my basement. I felt certain he was going to die. It was late and my vet's office was closed. I pleaded for God to save his life and called a good friend of mine for advice. She had an idea, and the necessary supplies, to possibly help him. I packed him up and took him to her house, and she gave him IV fluids. He perked up almost immediately and has been fine ever since. God saved my cat's life, but He used the knowledge and expertise of my friend.

I call this cat Ishmael. The meaning of that name is "the Lord hears." My little tabby is a constant reminder that God does hear and He does answer prayer.

Have you experienced a great answer to prayer? Give God the glory.

Thoughts on Psalm 108: The fall of Goliath was just the first of David's many victories in battle. Many times during his life, David had to fight the Philistines, and like Goliath they, too, fell before him. It is written, "Over Philistia will I triumph" (v. 9). The successes and victories David enjoyed throughout his life were due only to the goodness of God.

The last two verses are a heartfelt prayer to God. "Give us help from trouble: for vain is the help of man. Through God we shall do valiantly: for he it is that shall tread down our enemies" (vv. 12–13). This prayer should be the cry of every Christian. Almost every day we encounter some type of trouble, and only God can give the necessary help. As much as man may try to help, human assistance is paltry. David was encouraging us by reminding us that with God's help, we will do great things, for it is God who will destroy our enemies. May this psalm strengthen you today no matter what troubles you may encounter.

Prayer

Dear heavenly Father, thank You for Your answers to my prayers. Thank You for victories won, bodies healed, relationships restored, and needs of all kinds met. I know You use people to do Your will, but You are the One who is in control. Help me always to give You the credit for Your answers to my prayers. Thank You for all of the people You have used in my life to give me Your blessings. I pray You will use me in the lives of others to be a blessing to them. I ask this in the name of Christ. Amen.

— —

Day 5
David Behaves Himself Wisely

Daily Bible Reading: 1 Samuel 18 and Psalm 101

Today's Verse: "David behaved himself wisely in all his ways; and the Lord was with him." (1 Samuel 18:14)

Bible Lesson: Overnight, David went from being a virtual nobody to the most popular person in Saul's kingdom. King Saul, recognizing David's ability, would not let David leave his palace but made him captain over his men of war. Quickly enough, Saul's servants liked him, and the women praised David in their songs and dances. Even Saul's son, Jonathan, became David's loyal and faithful friend.

Unlike Jonathan, Saul became very jealous of David because he sensed the Lord had departed from him but was with David. It seems that because of David's fame and popularity, Saul realized David would be the next king, so Saul determined to get rid of him.

While he was still with Saul, David played the harp for him whenever an evil spirit, sent from God, came upon Saul. However, twice while David was playing the harp, Saul threw a javelin—a lightweight spear—at David in an attempt to pin him against the wall. Both times David escaped unharmed.

Saul's daughter, Princess Michal, loved David. Marriage to the daughter of the king was offered freely as part of the payment for killing Goliath. But Saul went back on his word and insisted that for a dowry, instead of money, David would have to kill one hundred uncircumcised, heathen Philistines. Saul thought this would be an ideal solution—not for David to prove his love for his daughter but for David to be killed by the Philistines.

Circumcision was the token of the covenant between God and the men of Israel, the symbol they were God's special and chosen people. The presentation of foreskins was obvious proof the enemy was dead! David accepted Saul's challenge, and with his men he killed not one hundred but rather two hundred Philistines, and he presented the required proof before the king.

In all of his dealings with King Saul and others, David conducted himself wisely. David established for himself a good reputation, a good testimony, and a good name.

Ponderings of a Woman after God's Heart: In 1 Samuel 18, we read four times that David behaved himself wisely. Every day we live, we behave, and our behavior is either wise or foolish. Behaving wisely is not easy, and it does not come naturally. Our flesh and sin nature wants to, and very often succeeds, in making us behave very foolishly. It is only by submitting ourselves to God and desiring His help that we can be wise in what we do.

You may find yourself in the depths of despair today, or things are going very well for you. No matter what is going on in your life, I encourage you to humbly ask God to help you in all of your dealings and decisions, and to be wise—both for yourself, personally, and for your testimony as a Christian.

David went above and beyond in his requested duty. Daily, you have a job to do. Actually, you probably have several jobs. Many times it may be true women work harder than men! Attempt to stand out above mediocrity, and go above and beyond the call of duty in all of your tasks, even the humble, daily, and mundane ones.

An encouraging verse in Ephesians says, "Knowing that whatsoever good thing any man doeth, the same shall he receive of the Lord, whether he be bond or free" (Ephesians 6:8). You are working for a heavenly Master who will reward you in a far greater way than you can imagine. Payday may not be until eternity, but strive every day to both behave and work wisely. Someday you will be glad you did.

Thoughts on Psalm 101: This psalm of David was written after he became king. Although David did not behave wisely in all aspects of his entire life, this was his desire. In this psalm, he gave us some very practical advice as to how to live wisely.

As king, he knew he needed to set a good example for all of his subjects. Good behavior must be modeled from the top down. In this psalm, he said, "I will walk within my house with a perfect heart" (v. 2). Even in the privacy of his home, David knew he needed to do what was right before God.

David purposed to totally eliminate all wicked influences, whether they were things or people, from his life. He went on to write that he would have nothing to do with slanderers and haughty people. David knew those who were wicked would influence him in a wicked way. He wisely desired to be surrounded by only good, faithful people.

David set a good example for every Christian woman to eliminate wicked influences from her life, whether they are things or people. Following the example of David in this psalm, you, too, will be on the right track of behaving yourself wisely.

Prayer

Dear heavenly Father, I know it is not in me to be able to behave myself wisely, so I am asking that You help me. Please give me Your wisdom in all I do each day. Help me to do my daily tasks exceptionally well, as unto You. I desire that Your name be glorified through all of my actions. I pray in the name of Jesus Christ. Amen.

— —

Day 6
David Flees to Samuel

Daily Bible Reading: 1 Samuel 19 and Psalm 59

Today's Verse: "David fled, and escaped, and came to Samuel to Ramah, and told him all that Saul had done to him. And he and Samuel went and dwelt in Naioth." (1 Samuel 19:18)

Bible Lesson: While David was living at his home with his princess wife, Michal, Saul was making plans and giving orders to both his son Jonathan, and all of his servants, to kill David.

Jonathan, David's friend and now his brother-in-law, sought out David to warn him his life was in danger. He also interceded with Saul by asking him to not kill David, since David did nothing but good to both him and all of Israel. Saul swore to lay off his murderous intent toward David.

When the nation was threatened again by the Philistines, David went to war and killed them "with a great slaughter" (v. 8). Soon after that victory, the evil spirit from the Lord came upon Saul again, and for the third time, Saul attempted to murder David with his javelin.

David escaped home to his wife, who told him to leave that night in order to save his life. She helped David slip through the window just in time, right before Saul's messengers came to kill David in his bed.

David fled to the prophet of God, Samuel, whose house was in Ramah, and David told him "all that Saul had done to him" (v. 18). The prophet Samuel was a very important man in David's life. He was the one who had anointed David with oil a short time earlier, signifying he would be the next king. After Samuel heard David's story, they both went to a school of the prophets in nearby Naioth—which was probably established and maintained by Samuel. Samuel knew David needed both encouragement and physical safety. It's safe to say the future king who was running for his life was a bit discouraged at this point.

While in Naioth, Saul's messengers, and eventually Saul himself, caught up to David and Samuel, but God's spirit protected them both in a wonderful way while allowing David to flee Naioth.

Ponderings of a Woman after God's Heart: Although David was in legitimate and deep trouble, the way he handled this trial is an example to all of us. He sought the advice of a seasoned man of God and told him everything. Then they went and met with other believers.

God has given us godly men who fill the calling of pastors, teachers, and evangelists. (Ephesians 4:11). God will always use His people. He established your local church and the people there, both men and women, under the direction of a pastor, to help and encourage God's people in times of distress.

Regularly attending a local church is vitally important to your spiritual well-being. Being involved in a local church will both help you when you have a need and as a support to others when they are having problems in their own lives.

With the technology of this day and age in which we live, it is easy to stay at home and attend "church" in the comfort of your pajamas. While you may be able to stream some fantastic preachers, this is not a substitute for regular attendance at a local church. David needed face time with Samuel, and both of them needed the physical presence and support of other believers.

You are no different—you need a local pastor and a local church family. If you don't have one, ask God to direct you to a church. He has told us to "forsake not the assembling of yourselves together" (Hebrews 10:25). Since this is a command of God, God will definitely provide you with a place of worship.

Thoughts on Psalm 59: David wrote this psalm when he had to flee for his life from his home in the palace, because King Saul had sent messengers to kill him. While David was busy escaping, he still made sure he had prayer time with God.

This psalm is David's recorded prayer in this particular time of distress. This psalm lets us know bad things do happen to good people. David was innocent of any wrongdoing, yet the king's henchmen were sent to kill him in his bed. David took comfort knowing he was innocent while he called upon God to punish his enemies.

When we know we have done all in our power to do what is right and we still have enemies, know that God is on the side of the righteous and He will defend us. God will protect His people, and in so doing will show the wicked there is a God who defends His own. May this psalm lift your spirits and build your faith in God when you do right but still feel totally defeated.

Prayer

Dear heavenly Father, thank You for knowing the need for a local church. I thank You for my church and my church family. Please give my pastor wisdom on a daily basis as he seeks to serve You and his congregation. Please give him Your wisdom as he prays, preaches, and counsels so You will be able to use him to meet our spiritual needs. Help me to invest in the lives of others in my church and to encourage them, even as I have needed their love and support. I ask this all in the wonderful name of Jesus Christ. Amen.

— —

Day 7
Jonathan Protects David

Daily Bible Reading: 1 Samuel 20 and Psalm 64

Today's Verse: (Jonathan speaking) "Thou shalt not only while yet I live shew me the kindness of the Lord, that I die not: But also, thou shalt not cut off thy kindness from my house for ever: no, not when the Lord hath cut off the enemies of David everyone from the face of the earth." (1 Samuel 20:14–15)

Bible Lesson: Yesterday, we left King Saul in a trance (1 Samuel 19). This God-arranged delay gave David the time he needed to return to the palace and to his friend Jonathan. It is interesting to observe that Saul's palace held both David's greatest ally and his worst enemy.

David fled to Jonathan to tell him what had transpired and to ask for his help in reconciling with his father, King Saul. Jonathan promised to help David; but not knowing for sure how the king felt about him, David requested permission from Jonathan to miss the celebration of a holy feast day and to hide himself until he was assured he would be safe near King Saul. Jonathan, who loved both his friend and his father, found it hard to believe his own father was intent on committing the crime of murder of a good and innocent man. Jonathan knew David would become the king of Israel, even though he, himself, was next in line for the throne. Jonathan was not at all jealous of David. He only made David promise that when David did become king that he would not kill Jonathan nor any of his family members. In ancient times, it was the practice for the new king to kill the family members, and even supporters, of the former king for protection against any revolt.

The next day Jonathan learned the bitter truth that his father was, indeed, intent on killing David, after King Saul attempted to kill Jonathan with the same javelin he had reserved for David. With a heavy heart, Jonathan found David and told him the news that he was no longer safe anywhere near King Saul.

The two best friends then had a tearful departure. Jonathan reminded David of the promise they had made each other and directed David again to the Lord God Jehovah. No doubt this was also intended to remind and encourage David that he was promised the throne. As Jonathan returned to the city, David began the life of an outlaw.

Ponderings of a Woman after God's Heart: Bad things happen to good people. David was to be the next king of Israel, yet he was now running for his life, although totally innocent of any wrongdoing. His trials were allowed by God to refine him and to teach him valuable lessons.

You may be facing a trial as you read this devotional. You may have financial distress, be facing the possible loss of a loved one, or have some serious health problems. Just because you have difficulties in your life does not necessarily mean God's hand of chastisement is upon you. David had done nothing wrong; in fact, he was doing everything right, yet he was forced to flee from his home and live the life of an outlaw because the king of the land wanted him dead.

Keep in mind that just because you are obedient to God, it does not mean He will keep you from troubles. One preacher aptly said, "When you are right with God, don't expect a new car. Rather, expect God to blow up the one you have." As unfair as this may seem to us, God has a reason for sending trouble our way. When we know we are serving God and doing right by Him, we can be assured God has allowed our troubles to be a test, not a punishment. Trials are designed to bring us closer to God, as we learn to depend on Him in an even greater way.

Thoughts on Psalm 64: Do you ever feel you are trying to live a righteous life but you are getting slandered by wicked people? David felt like this, and he penned this psalm about those who were plotting to kill him.

Although you may not have people wishing you dead, you may have those who talk evil about you behind your back. David encouraged both himself back then, and us today, in this wonderful psalm that describes slanderers and what God will do to them.

David wrote that those who use their tongue to speak evil against the perfect (those innocent of the charges being made against them) are shooting arrows—bitter words. He also wrote that God will use this same type of weapon against them. God will wound their tongue so everyone will know this is God's doing. The righteous and the upright in heart will be glad in this work of the Lord against those who speak evil.

In an indirect way, this psalm is also a warning to not speak badly about people. Despite what you may think about others, don't slander them. Today, ask God to help you use your tongue to encourage other people to love God more.

Prayer

Dear heavenly Father, thank You for my friends. I know You are my best friend. I know that when you allow trials in my life, they are meant to make me stronger. Help me in my troubles to go to You first, but I also thank You for giving me friends to help me through these trials. Help me also to be a loving support to my friends when they need my encouragement, and let me be like Jonathan when I point others to You. I pray in the name of precious Jesus. Amen.

— —

Day 8
David Gets Goliath's Sword

Daily Bible Reading: 1 Samuel 21:1–9 and Psalm 31

Today's Verse: "The priest said, The sword of Goliath the Philistine, whom thou slewest in the valley of Elah, behold, it is here wrapped in a cloth behind the ephod: if thou wilt take that, take it: for there is no other save that here. And David said, There is none like that; give it me." (1 Samuel 21:9)

Bible Lesson: David began the life of an outlaw, running for his life from King Saul. Three days into his journey, David and the men who had followed him stopped at the city of Nob to ask Ahimelech, the priest of God, for some food and other supplies.

David met with Ahimelech alone. The priest did not know there was a serious falling out between David and King Saul. He was also a bit afraid when David appeared, obviously in a hurry, and requested supplies and weapons. David lied to Ahimelech about why he was there, only telling him he was on a special and hasty assignment for King Saul.

The only bread Ahimelech said was available to David was the shewbread—loaves of unleavened bread that representing the twelve tribes of Israel. It was baked once a week and laid out before the Lord, and this holy bread was only for the priests to eat. David demanded that Ahimelech give him this bread, but Ahimelech hesitated because never before had a non-priest eaten the shewbread. David was well aware of this fact, but he had a great need. Ahimelech, after making sure the bodies of David and those with him were at least in some part undefiled, allowed David to have this special bread. Many years later, Jesus, the Son of David, referred to this event. He said David needed the food, and that under these unusual circumstances, Ahimelech did the right thing in giving David the holy bread (Mark 2:25–26).

David then asked if Ahimelech had any weaponry. The only thing Ahimelech had to offer David was Goliath's sword, which was most likely kept as a souvenir—a tangible reminder of how God saved the Israelites. David eagerly took Goliath's sword, but it is not recorded he ever used it. Ahimelech was sure he was helping his king by assisting David. However, Doeg, a servant of Saul, was there also and saw and heard everything that transpired between David and Ahimelech.

Ponderings of a Woman after God's Heart: Trials are times of temptation. For David, running for his life from Saul was a trial; he was tempted to lie and he did. David was in deep trouble and he really needed some help. Going to the priest of God was a good thing; David asked for and received physical things. However, he did not ask for any spiritual help.

Don't put your trust in physical things only. We are physical entities living in a physical world, but we are spiritual beings too. During every day of our lives, we have both physical and spiritual needs. David came to the spiritual man of God, but he only requested and received physical blessings. He neglected the spiritual aspect completely, although he was in a place where he could have and should have obtained both. While we do all in our power to meet our physical needs, we must also remember not to neglect the equally important aspect of spiritual needs.

Every day we feed ourselves and attend to our hygienic wants and needs, and these are good and necessary things. In a similar manner, we cannot allow our spiritual part to be empty. Here are some important ways to meet our vital spiritual needs:

- Confessing our sins to God (ideally as they occur)
- Asking for God's help and His wisdom daily
- Daily Bible reading
- Regularly attending a local church
- Taking communion

- Fellowshipping with other Christians
- Praying for both our needs and the needs of others
- Proclaiming God's goodness

Thoughts on Psalm 31: David wrote this psalm in a time of deep distress. He was praying because he had a strong confidence in God's help based on times past. Now David was asking earnestly for God's deliverance from his present troubles.

In his prayer, David reminded God how he hates evil and how God had helped him in the past. This psalm is a mixture of petitioning God and praising God. It is a good example to all of us in our times of trouble to ask for help while remembering and praising God for answers to prayers in times past.

It is precious to know that God is very near to His children when they cry out to Him. We really do have a very present help in times of trouble.

Prayer

Dear heavenly Father, thank You that You are the source of all physical and spiritual blessings. Every day I need both, and You are so good to provide. Thank You for the people you have given me who help me both physically and spiritually. Let me be a similar blessing to them. I pray and ask this in the name of Your Son, Jesus Christ.

– –

Day 9
David Cares for His Parents

Daily Bible Reading: 1 Samuel 21:10–15; 22:1–5 and Psalm 34

Today's Verse: "Every one that was in distress, and every one that was in debt, and every one that was discontented, gathered themselves unto him; and he became a captain over them: and there were with him about four hundred men." (1 Samuel 22:2)

Bible Lesson: David needed a place to stay, but not in Saul's country. As a fugitive, he headed to Gath, the very place Goliath was from.

The king of Gath was Achish. The servants of Achish were nervous that David and his men were in their area. Not only had he killed their most fearsome warrior Goliath, but David also had the reputation of killing "ten thousands" (1 Samuel 21:11). Contrariwise, David was fearful they would kill him since he was a mighty warrior. To show he had no designs on killing anyone in Gath, and fearing for his own life, David pretended to be out of his mind—insanity. Achish tolerated this seemingly crazy man but only for a short time. He even joined in with his servants by making fun of David. But since an insane man was more of a bother than anything else, Achish sent David away from his kingdom.

David and his men hid in the cave of Adullam, which is a Hebrew word meaning "refuge." This was a stronghold near the town of Adullam, also referred to as "the hold." Here David composed the wonderful Psalm 34.

God sent people to David while he was in the stronghold. Among the first group that came to hide out with David was his family. His three oldest brothers were serving in Saul's army; but since they were related to David, no doubt they, too, feared for their lives. The others who came to him were those in distress, in debt, and discontented.

David became a captain of more than four hundred of these less-than-desirable men.

Most of the people who joined themselves unto David were strong, able-bodied men. The exception was David's parents—his father was considered an old man at that time (1 Samuel 17:12). For their protection and comfort, David's parents were not to rough it like the others, so he made arrangements for them to live with the king of Moab. The king of Moab may have been related to David, since Jesse was the grandson of Ruth the Moabititess. David's parents lived in Moab while David camped out in the cave of Adullam.

After David lived in the hold for some time, the prophet Gad came with a message that God wanted David to return to the country of Judah. When David returned home to Judah, he took not only his four hundred men but his parents also.

Ponderings of a Woman after God's Heart: David made his parents his first priority. Even though David had seven older brothers and at least one sister, it was David who made the necessary arrangements for his parents. David obeyed the Law of Moses which read, "Honor thy father and thy mother: that thy days may be long upon the land which the Lord thy God giveth thee" (Exodus 20:12).

Let me encourage you today to honor your parents and make them a priority while you still have them. I know it is far easier to care for an infant than it is to care for an elderly adult. Your parents gave you life; do as much as you can to give life back to them. This can include physical help, financial relief, and/or spiritual encouragement.

My mother was a wonderful example of this. My grandmother had Alzheimer's disease for many years, which progressively got worse as time went on. Refusing to put her in a nursing home, my mother, not a nurse by any means, bravely took on the major responsibility of caring for her at home. Because of my mother's care, my grandmother was able to pass away in the comfort of her own home.

Care of an elderly parent can be very trying and in some ways unrewarding, yet after they are gone, you will not have any regrets. I believe taking care of your parents is a means of laying up treasures in heaven. Many years after David provided for his parents, his son Solomon penned this holy command, "Hearken unto thy father that begat thee, and despise not thy mother when she is old" (Proverbs 23:22).

Thoughts on Psalm 34: This psalm is a joyful and triumphant song of praise to God for His deliverance of David. It reads similarly to a five-star product review on Amazon. The happy customer, in this case David, was praising God for His goodness and His help.

Specifically, God delivered David from all of his fears. He was not ashamed to trust in God because God was dependable. He was poor, but the Lord saved him from all of his troubles, and he had the divine protection of the angel of the Lord.

David excitedly called to children to teach them the fear of the Lord in order that they would experience happiness and long life. He went on to tell of the privileges of the righteous versus those of evildoers. He concluded this psalm of praise with the promise that "none of them that trust in him [God] shall be desolate" (v. 22).

Prayer

Dear heavenly Father, thank You for my parents. Help me to help them as long as they live. In honor of my parents, I desire and need Your help to live a godly life that would be pleasing to both You and them. I ask this in the Savior's name. Amen.

— —

Day 10
Massacre of Faithful Priests

Daily Bible Reading: 1 Samuel 22:6–23 and Psalm 52

Today's Verse: "Ahimelech answered the king, and said, And who is so faithful among all thy servants as David, which is the king's son in law, and goeth at thy bidding, and is honorable in thine house?" (1 Samuel 22:14)

Bible Lesson: In yesterday's lesson we learned the prophet Gad counseled David to return to the land of Judah, and Saul was told David was back in his country. Saul then complained to his men that none of them would help him find and kill David. Furthermore, he accused them all of conspiring against him and siding with David. Then Doeg, the Edomite, spoke up. He told Saul he saw David with Ahimelech, the priest of the Lord, in Nob.

Saul pounced on this bit of information and immediately summoned Ahimelech and all of the other priests. After Ahimelech admitted to what he did in helping David, stating his innocence because he had no idea of the falling out between the king and David, Saul gave the order to have all of the priests of the Lord slain. Saul's footmen would not obey this unreasonable order to kill the priests since they obviously had the fear of God in them. They also realized these men of God were innocent of any wrongdoing. Doeg, the Edomite, had no such qualms. At Saul's order, Doeg murdered Ahimelech and eighty-four other godly priests. He continued his killing spree at Nob, the city of the priests, wiping out all of their families and even their livestock. No doubt Saul rewarded Doeg very handsomely for this heinous act.

Ahimelech's son, Abiathar, managed to escape and ran to David. David was heartsick when he heard the terrible news as he was partly to blame for the death of all of the priests because of his lie to Ahimelech. Perhaps if David had been truthful with Ahimelech, the priests could have taken precautions against Saul. But all David could do now was welcome Abiathar and assure him he would be safe. Though his heart was heavy, David knew these faithful men and women were in paradise. He composed the wonderful Psalm 52 in honor of all those brave souls.

Ponderings of a Woman after God's Heart: So many times it seems evil is rewarded, sin is glorified, and goodness is marginalized. These men of God and their families became martyrs, and from a purely physical standpoint, this was a terrible tragedy. Persecution of Christian believers has happened throughout history and continues into our present day. It is easy to get angry with God when we do not understand what He is allowing.

In Psalm 52, David gives us a glimpse of God's mind. David truly had a grasp of eternity, and he shared that with us in this psalm. He wrote that God would take men like the evil Doeg and "root him out of the land of the living" (Psalm 52:2). Unrepentant evildoers have only the everlasting fires of hell—never-ending death—in their future. However, the righteous ones, those who trusted God while they were alive but lost their lives to Doeg's sword that day, were just fine. They were not really destroyed. They went through the door of death and were welcomed with their loved ones into Abraham's bosom. They received a crown of life (Revelation 2:10).

Let me encourage you to put your trust in God, no matter what tragedy or evil you may hear about. Remember that if not in this life, then for all of eternity, God has promised that "When all the workers of iniquity do flourish; it is that they shall be destroyed for ever" (Psalm 95:7).

Thoughts on Psalm 52: In this psalm, David is angry at the wicked—like the evil and boastful Doeg. There were and always will be people like Doeg. These evildoers delight in stirring up trouble and using their tongues to ruin the righteous. They may succeed, just like Doeg did, but God is still in control. Of such people, David wrote that God will destroy them, and when this judgment comes upon the wicked, the righteous will rejoice. God is a God of vengeance, as He said, "I will render vengeance to mine enemies" (Deuteronomy 32:41), and when He does, those who are righteous will see just how very foolish the wicked really were.

David contrasted the evil ones who will be totally destroyed by God to those who are righteous. David described himself as a "green olive tree" (v. 8), giving the idea of being firmly planted, rooted, settled, flourishing, and bearing fruit—all within God's house. Remember David and his reactions when you see or hear of unsettling events and evil people. Purpose to be like David: trust in God, serve God, be found in the house of God, and you, too, will enjoy stability despite troubling times.

Prayer

Dear heavenly Father, please restrain the evil and wickedness in the world today. I know that just as wicked men delight in wickedness, so, too, do You delight in goodness. Help me, like David, to rejoice and to be glad for Your goodness and for Your promise that You will surely, someday, destroy both evil and evildoers. In the meantime, please help me to trust in You in an even greater way. I pray this all in Christ's name. Amen.

— —

Day 11
David Delivers Keilah from the Philistines

Daily Bible Reading: 1 Samuel 23: 1–14 and Psalm 143

Today's Verse: "David's men said unto him, Behold, we be afraid here in Judah: how much more then if we come to Keilah against the armies of the Philistines?" (1 Samuel 23:3)

Bible Lesson: David returned to Judah on the advice of the prophet Gad, where he found work to do. The Philistines had invaded Judah and were robbing food from the threshing floors of the Israelites living in the city of Keilah. David was given this news with the unspoken request, "Do something to save us!" David wisely consulted God as to whether or not he should go and kill the marauding bands of Philistines. God told him to go. After David gave the order to his band of now six hundred men, some had a legitimate concern: They were all hiding from Saul, and if they went to Keilah, word would get back to Saul as to their whereabouts. David again consulted the Lord. Again, God told him to go, adding the encouraging promise, "I will deliver the Philistines into thine hand" (1 Samuel 23:4).

At Keilah, David and his men had a great victory and saved the inhabitants of the city, but Saul found out where David was, which greatly pleased him. He, in his twisted mind, gave God the glory for trapping David in a city with "gates and bars" (v. 7).

Abiathar, the priest of the Lord, had an ephod—an object used by Old Testament priests to determine God's will. David asked the priest to consult the ephod to determine if he was safe in Keilah from Saul. David asked two very specific things of God: Would Saul come to Keilah to try to kill him and would the men of Keilah deliver David and his men into the hand of Saul? God's answer to both of David's questions was yes, so David and his men left the comfort and security of Keilah to go into hiding again.

Ponderings of a Woman after God's Heart: The lesson we learn here from David is to consult God before every decision we make, both large and small. Be it a new job, a plan of action, marriage, a financial decision, and so on, God needs to be both consulted and obeyed.

Obviously we don't have a priest with an ephod to determine God's will for our lives, but in His love for us, God has given us tools that are just as powerful that can be used in all of the decisions we need to make. They are these:

- **The Word of God:** What does the Bible have to say about the decision you want to make? Suppose you have an opportunity to team up with a non-Christian lady to start a business, but the Bible warns about being "unequally yoked together with unbelievers" (2 Corinthians 6:14). A partnership is a yoke, so going into business with a non-Christian is against God's will.

- **The Spirit of God:** Suppose the Bible doesn't have anything in particular to say about what you are considering. Pray and ask God to guide you with His Holy Spirit. Jesus promised the guidance of the Holy Spirit when He said, "Howbeit when he, the Spirit of truth, is come, he will guide you into all truth" (John 16:13). As you pray about the decision you need to make, let God's spirit speak to your heart concerning what He would have you do. Be very careful you do not override the quiet voice of God with your own strong desires.

- **The Circumstances of God:** God opens and closes doors of opportunity. Here is a simple example: you want to buy a pair of new shoes. There is nothing in the Word of God saying you should not buy these shoes. You pray and feel that God's spirit is not directing you away from these shoes, so you go to Amazon and click on the shoes, only to discover your size is sold out. The circumstances of God are such that you cannot complete your purchase.

Consistently using these tools will help you in finding the perfect will of God.

Thoughts on Psalm 143: Did you ever feel a great need for direction in your life? David did. This psalm is David's plea to God to guide him when he didn't know what to do. This is a good psalm to read and meditate upon when you need some personal guidance. Today you may need direction to mend your marriage, continue at your workplace, help your children, or do something in any other area of your life. When you don't know what to do, you need to go to God and ask for His help.

In verse 8 there is both a plea to God for help and a piece of practical advice: David wrote, "Cause me to hear thy loving kindness in the morning." David wanted to start his day with God's direction so he had it for the entire day. This is a good practice for us too. We need to ask for God's guidance in the morning and trust and follow Him for every decision throughout that day. This simple but powerful practice should be repeated each day for the rest of our lives.

A good thing to do when you have a decision to make is to pray God will prevent you from doing anything you may later regret. Ask God for His leading; He alone knows the future and wants the very best for you.

Prayer

Dear heavenly Father, thank You for Your perfect will for my life. Thank You for giving me the tools to determine Your will. Help me to consistently use them to closely follow You in all of my life's decisions.

I pray this in the name that is above all names: Christ Jesus.

Day 12

David and Jonathan in the Wilderness of Ziph

Daily Bible Reading: 1 Samuel 23:15, 29 and Psalm 110

Today's Verse: "Jonathan Saul's son arose, and went to David into the wood, and strengthened his hand in God. And he said unto him, Fear not: for the hand of Saul my father shall not find thee; and thou shalt be king over Israel, and I shall be next unto thee; and that also Saul my father knoweth." (1 Samuel 23:16–17)

Bible Lesson: The shining star of this passage is not David but his friend Jonathan. David and his men were hiding from Saul. They were camping out, setting watch, and continually on guard in the wilderness of Ziph. Many of David's men were possibly wondering when this time of running would finally end. David himself was discouraged. Perhaps he was wondering if he would ever be king. Was Samuel mistaken? Did David hear him correctly so long ago?

Then, when David needed it most, his friend Jonathan came to strengthen David's hand in God. He told him that even though his father, King Saul, was intent on killing David, he would not find him. David would someday be king over the land and Jonathan would be his second in command. They renewed their covenant, the promise they had made before—that when David became king, he would not kill Jonathan's family.

Jonathan gave David priceless but intangible spiritual and emotional gifts, exactly what David needed to meet his deepest needs. Here are the comforting words Jonathan gave to David:

"Fear not." Jonathan brought peace. He was not there to spy out David's position for his dad.

"For the hand of Saul my father shall not find thee." Jonathan reminded David of God's protection over him.

"And thou shalt be king over Israel." God will fulfill His word.

"And I shall be next unto thee." David could always count on Jonathan's support.

Then Jonathan left David in the wilderness and returned to his house. Encouraged and strengthened by the words of Jonathan, David got the needed psychological strength that gave him an extra burst of stamina to rally his men for the next round of the deadly cat-and-mouse game with Saul.

The men of Ziph knew David was in the area, and they were only too eager to give him up to Saul. David fled to another wilderness, this time a place called Maon. At one point in Maon, only a mountain separated David from Saul; David was on one side of the mountain and Saul on the other. David was almost in Saul's reach, but before Saul could surround David, he received a message that his attention was immediately needed back home because of a Philistine invasion. After this narrow escape from Saul, David retreated to the strongholds of Engedi.

Ponderings of a Woman after God's Heart: The three verses that record the last meeting between David and Jonathan show the beauty of Christian friendship. So many times my mother would happily exclaim, "My friends, I am so thankful for my friends! What would I do without them?" Then she would ask me, "Have you talked with some of your friends recently?" My mother knew the priceless value of having good friends.

While Jonathan did not give David anything tangible such as provisions or money, nor, better yet, the calling off of his father from trying to kill him, Jonathan gave David what he needed most—encouragement to continue to serve the Lord and to stay alive, because Jonathan knew David would be the next king so he had to live.

At this time in David's life, staying alive was hard work, and he needed encouragement. Jonathan's words to David could be summed up with the words, "Be ye strong therefore and let not your hands be weak: for your work shall be rewarded" (2 Chronicles 15:7). Sometimes, well-spoken words are more valuable than gold and silver. David's son Solomon observed "A word fitly spoken is like apples of gold in pictures of silver" (Proverbs 25:11).

Our Christian friends are gifts from God to help meet our spiritual and emotional needs. Godly friends are a very precious blessing from God Himself. True Christian friends want only the best for us, and they will assist us in our daily walk with the Lord. They bring us the priceless gifts of godly encouragement, prayer, a listening ear, a caring heart, godly counsel, and many other similar benefits.

So now you know what your Christian friends can do for you, let me encourage you to strive to strengthen your friends' hands in God. Friendship is a two-way street. While you depend on your friends for help, remember and strive to be a good and encouraging friend to them also. Pray for your friends. Remind your friends of God's goodness and of His promises, and encourage them to draw closer to the Lord in their daily lives and trials. This is truly being a good friend.

Thoughts on Psalm 110: In this triumphant psalm about a reigning king, David gave Jehovah God all the glory. Whether David wrote this psalm while he was still running for his life from Saul or after he was king, the strength of the king in this psalm is only because of God, and David is careful to give God the glory.

David knew that someday he would be king and his work would be rewarded. He also knew any success he would enjoy was only because of God's grace and help. Although David was running for his life, he knew God had promised to give him victory over all of his enemies and would do it.

Prayer

Dear heavenly Father, thank You for giving me friends. Thank You for using them to help me meet my emotional, spiritual, and sometimes even physical needs. I humbly ask that You will give each of my friends a very special blessing today. Help me to be a good friend to them in return. Help me, like Jonathan, to continually point my friends to You so they may know You are the very best Friend anyone could have. I pray in the Savior's name. Amen.

− −

Day 13
David Spares Saul in Engedi

Daily Bible Reading: 1 Samuel 24 and Psalm 25

Today's Verse: "He said unto his men, The Lord forbid that I should do this thing unto my master, the Lord's anointed, to stretch forth mine hand against him, seeing he is the anointed of the Lord." (1 Samuel 24:6)

Bible Lesson: After a brief respite, Saul again began to hunt David, intent on killing him. Saul's faithful spies informed him David was in Engedi. Saul, with his army of three thousand men, went searching for David and his small band of fewer than one thousand followers. When Saul needed to excuse himself to "cover his feet" (today we would say "use the bathroom"), he went alone into a cave in Engedi for necessary privacy. Saul thought he was alone in the cave, but he had unwittingly chosen the very cave where David and his men were hiding!

Having Saul so close at hand, vulnerable and alone, seemed like a God-given opportunity for David and his men to kill their enemy. Saul, not realizing he was not alone, removed his robe to keep it clean while he was relieving himself. David refused to kill Saul, but he cut off a portion of Saul's coat instead. David's conscience then bothered him that he'd even ruined Saul's garment (v. 11), so he followed Saul out of the cave and respectfully addressed Saul as "my lord the king" before bowing before him and apologizing for what he had done. He referred to Saul as "God's anointed" (v. 10). David sought to set Saul straight by telling him he didn't want to harm him. Despite Saul's intentions toward David, David had these words of wisdom for Saul: "The Lord avenge me of thee: but mine hand shall not be upon thee" (v. 12)

David's humble speech moved Saul to tears. He recognized he was in the wrong and admitted that David was more righteous than he. He further admitted that he knew David would be the next king and begged David to spare the lives of his family members. Accordingly,

David promised this to Saul. After this exchange Saul went home, but David remained in the wilderness.

Ponderings of a Woman after God's Heart: Had Saul found David alone and unarmed, things might have been far different. David was, and had every right to be, angry with Saul. David trusted that God would not only take care of him but that He would also punish Saul. When he said, "The Lord avenge me of thee," he knew the sobering truth and reassuring promise of Romans 12:19: "Vengeance is mine; I will repay, saith the Lord."

God is the sole owner of all vengeance. The word "vengeance" means punishment that is inflicted for an injury or wrong, or retribution. This powerful action belongs exclusively to God. It is His alone, not ours. God knows there is a need in this world for vengeance; however, as angry as we may get or whatever opportunity we may have to execute well-deserved revenge, doing it ourselves is actually stealing from God something that exclusively belongs to Him.

God not only communicates He has the sole ownership of this powerful act, but He also promises He will use it to repay evil, and on those who inflict it. God Almighty, who is a God of love, is also a God of wrath. He will bring powerful punishment on those who have hurt His children. God has promised to not only take care of us but to "take care" of our enemies also.

Although God's timing is not our timing, He will repay evildoers far better than we can. David had to wait for God to avenge him of Saul, but eventually God did. You may be suffering something from someone today, and you may have every reason to be angry at the treatment you are getting; but keep this in mind: God sees all and He remembers. Wait on God to avenge you of your enemies; God always keeps His word.

Thoughts on Psalm 57: Many times, the Bible uses the phrase "it came to pass." We sometimes say during hard times, "This, too, shall pass." David said something similar: "Until these calamities be overpast" (Psalm 57:1). David knew his troubles of running for his life from Saul would someday be over, but during the time of his calamities, he penned this wonderful psalm. Here, he comforted himself with the knowledge that he had put his trust in God and God alone to deliver him.

This psalm is a wonderful reminder that during our trials, we have one sure shelter—the protection of God. David set a great example for all of us. He was determined, his heart was fixed, and he would sing and give praise to God, even during his most frustrating, perilous times. I hope you remember this example of David and determine to both trust and praise God during all of your trials.

Prayer

Dear heavenly Father, thank You for Your wonderful promise of taking vengeance upon those who hurt me. Keep me from stealing from You when I am tempted to take matters into my own hands. Please remind me that You have promised to repay those who do me wrong, and I know You always keep Your promises. Thank You for Your protection over me, Your child. I ask this in Your Son's name.

Amen.

--

Day 14
Abigail Captures David's Heart

Daily Bible Reading: 1 Samuel 25 and Psalm 128

Today's Verse: "The name of the man was Nabal; and the name of his wife Abigail: and she was a woman of good understanding, and of a beautiful countenance." (1 Samuel 25:3)

Bible Lesson: Someone once said the story of David and Abigail is the sexiest romance in the Bible. The chapter opens by introducing a wealthy farmer, Nabal, and his wife, Abigail. Abigail is described as "a woman of good understanding," but her husband was "churlish and evil in his doings" (v. 3).

David and his men took it upon themselves to help Nabal during sheep shearing season by protecting both Nabal's sheep and his shepherds. In return, David asked for much needed provisions. David assumed that if they helped the locals, the locals would help them; however, Nabal refused to help David and his men. When David heard of Nabal's refusal, he was angry and ready to kill. In a rage, he took four hundred men to wipe out Nabal and all that pertained to him, and also to raid the place to get the necessary supplies.

One of Nabal's servants found out they were about to be invaded and killed by David and his men. Nabal's servants described their boss as "a son of Belial." This phrase indicates a person who is a son of the devil, one who is devoid of the Lord. The servants also seemed to be afraid to tell Nabal he was in trouble, so they told Abigail instead.

Abigail, knowing her husband not only was slated for death but also all of the servants and herself, quickly gathered provisions and took them and her servants to mollify David. When she met David face-to-face, her words were truly those of a wise woman. She sincerely apologized for the foolish actions of her husband, saying he really was a fool. She humbly gave the Lord credit for preventing David from needless bloodshed. She further told David she knew what was going on between him and Saul, but also knew God would make David ruler over all Israel. She concluded by asking for a blessing from David once he became king.

David graciously accepted her presents and told her her actions had saved her household from certain destruction. The next day, Abigail told her husband all she had done concerning David. Nabal was so disturbed by what he was told "that his heart died within him, and he became as a stone" (v. 37). About ten days later, God killed Nabal. David, learning about Nabal's death, wasted no time in sending a messenger to ask Abigail to become his wife, and she immediately accepted.

Ponderings of a Woman after God's Heart: As women, we can all learn something from Abigail, the woman who captured the heart of the future king. Here are some highlights of her speech that we can use in our daily communication:

She was a believer in the Lord God of Israel. She mentioned the Lord six times in her speech to David.

She wanted the best for David's future—to be king of Israel.

She was humble. It was because of her wise actions that David did not kill Nabal, his family, and his servants; yet she gave God the credit.

She asked for a blessing.

Ladies, let me encourage you in your everyday interactions with your husband, your children, your boss, your pastor, and all of your friends to imitate the gentle wisdom and wise words of Abigail. Ask God daily to give you kind words to speak and an understanding heart. Try to pattern your speech in a similar fashion to that of Abigail. Let your speech proclaim the goodness of God. Use your tongue to encourage others to serve God in a greater way. Don't talk about yourself, and don't be afraid to ask for a blessing.

Thoughts on Psalm 128: Psalms of degrees are traveling psalms. This is a happy, almost lighthearted psalm, yet it teaches some important truths. Visualize the ancient Israelites singing this psalm with joy on their faces as they traveled to worship in Jerusalem. These words are encouraging, peaceful, and comforting.

David began this psalm with the words, "Blessed is everyone that feareth the Lord; that walketh in his ways" (v. 1). To fear God is not to be afraid of Him but rather to be afraid to displease Him and disobey Him—by sinning and by not following His commandments and His ways. Being afraid to sin against God will result in your happiness and blessing.

In verse 6, David described a loving, peaceful, and comforting family scene; the man's wife is compared to a fruitful vine and his children as olive plants. The man who fears the Lord will lead his family in the way of blessing and happiness. The blessings promised to the man (or woman) who walks in the ways of the Lord continue with the promise of long life, grandchildren, and peaceful days.

Prayer

Dear heavenly Father, I thank You that You made me a woman. Help me to daily seek Your wisdom so that I, too, may have the reputation of being a woman of good understanding. Please give me wisdom in all of my works as a wife, mother, daughter, friend, and employee, knowing I am a reflection of You. Help me to glorify You in all I say, in all of my relationships, so You can use me to draw others closer to You.
In Jesus's name I pray. Amen.

– –

Day 15
David Spares Saul's Life Again

Daily Bible Reading: 1 Samuel 26 and Psalm 94

Today's Verse: "I pray thee, let my lord the king hear the words of his servant. If the Lord have stirred thee up against me, let him accept an offering: but if they be the children of men, cursed be they before the Lord." (1 Samuel 26:19)

Bible Lesson: David was still in the wilderness of Ziph. When Saul found out, he took three thousand men with him to find and kill David. This time, David changed his tactics and decided to confront Saul instead of running.

At night, when Saul and all of his men were in a deep sleep caused by God, David and his nephew Abishai went into the camp—all the way to Saul's bed. Abishai thought this was a God-given opportunity to kill Saul, but David stopped Abishai's deadly intent. David told him Saul's time to die would come but it was not for them to kill him. Instead, David and Abishai took Saul's spear and his cruse of water and escaped.

After David was quite a distance away, he called out to Abner, Saul's captain, and mocked him, stating there were people there to destroy Saul and that he, Abner, was not protecting his master. Saul, awakened by this exchange, addressed David; and just like the last time, Saul repented, saying, "I have sinned" (v. 21). He promised David that if he came back home, Saul would not kill him since David spared his life again.

Ponderings of a Woman after God's Heart: What was David thinking as he gazed down on Saul that night? Was he tempted to kill him? It's possible. Was he being jealous? Perhaps. Here was Saul—the anointed of the Lord. He had everything David did not have. He had a palace for a home, good food, a comfortable bed, and an army of men. However, David, too, was the anointed of the Lord, but unlike Saul he had no home. He lived in the wilderness and was always on guard, for one slip could mean death. It was difficult for him to trust anyone. He and his men lived by finding food wherever they could, and they often camped outside on the cold, hard ground. But no matter what David's negative thoughts were, he had to be strong and above reproach; he had to do right. God was watching, and Abishai was with him.

Ever feel similarly to David? Perhaps you try so hard to do what is right, to be above reproach in all of your ways, but you find it so difficult, especially when you see others who, according to the Bible, are doing wrong while appearing to be blessed at the same time.

If you can relate to this, then please read on. Remember Saul's parting words to David: "Thou shalt both do great things, and also shalt still prevail" (1 Samuel 26:25). David did what was right and he did prevail. Let Saul's words be an encouragement to you too. Keep doing what you know is right and you, too, will prevail.

Maybe David had this incident with Saul in his mind as he penned the comforting and encouraging words of Psalm 37 as an old man. Maybe he looked back on the times of his life when he was discouraged and said to all those who would read it, "Wait on the Lord, and keep his way, and he shall exalt thee to inherit the land: when the wicked are cut off, thou shalt see it" (v. 34). Let me also encourage you to keep the way of the Lord.

Thoughts on Psalm 94: Have you ever been persecuted for doing what was right? If you have, good for you! In 2 Timothy 3:12, we read, "Yea, and all that will live godly in Christ Jesus shall suffer persecution." This psalm is an encouragement for those who are being persecuted by sinful people. David gives the righteous both a voice and a wonderful hope in this psalm. He addressed the Lord God as the One who owns vengeance, imploring Him to judge and reward evildoers. He went on to describe what the wicked were doing to his people.

Instead of dwelling on the negative, David affirmed that God would not forsake His people; he recounted how the Lord helped him in the past. Despite all of the unrest about him, David wrote, "In the multitude of my thoughts within me thy comforts delight my soul" (v. 19).

Allow God to use this psalm to delight your soul in times of persecution, especially as you read the triumphant promise referring to persecutors: "And he [God] shall bring upon them their own iniquity and shall cut them off in their own wickedness; yea, the Lord our God shall cut them off" (v. 23).

Prayer

Dear heavenly Father, please help me do what is right, even when so many around me are doing wrong. Please help me to be above reproach, even when I feel what I am doing is stupid and I don't yet see Your blessings. Help me to trust in You, and please help me to prevail. In Christ's name I pray. Amen.

- -

Day 16
Send David Home

Daily Bible Reading: 1 Samuel 28:1–2; 29:1–11 and Psalm 56

Today's Verse: "Achish answered and said to David, I know that thou art good in my sight, as an angel of God: notwithstanding the princes of the Philistines have said, He shall not go up with us to the battle." (1 Samuel 29:9)

Bible Lesson: David, his men, and their families settled in the Philistines' land in the city of Ziklag. There, David was safe from Saul and had the protection, confidence, and respect of the Philistine king Achish for a year and four months (1 Samuel 27:7). The Philistines David allied himself with were preparing to go to war again with the Israelites, led by Saul. This was to be a great and serious battle, and Achish expected David to go with him and fight against his people for the Philistines.

Obviously, David found himself in a quandary. There was no way he could fight against Saul and his own people. He would be fighting against Jonathan's army, and there would be a chance he would even find himself in battle against Jonathan. Even though David was in the land of the Philistines, his heart was with his people, the Israelites. As the future king of Israel, he knew he must leave Achish and return to his own land.

In preparation for battle, the armies presented their troops before the heads of the Philistines. David and his men were with Achish, who was, no doubt, thrilled for the chance to fight alongside the famous Israelite warrior.

The lords of the Philistines saw David's men were among their troops and they were not happy. Even though Achish assured them David would be more than an asset to their cause, the other lords were not so sure. They felt that perhaps in the heat of battle, David's sympathies would be with his people; and because of this he would turn against the Philistines. Their fear was that David would cut off their heads instead in order to be reconciled to his former master, King Saul.

To keep up the act, David protested. Embarrassed, Achish told David and his men to return to Ziklag. There is no doubt that David returned to Ziklag rejoicing and thanking God for sparing him from fighting against his own people.

Ponderings of a Woman after God's Heart: Although this passage does not mention prayer, I believe David was doing a lot of praying and pleading with God to deliver him from this very sticky situation. God answered his prayers in a wonderful way.

Both history and the present are filled with remarkable answers to the prayers of God's people. Perhaps you have heard of wonderful answers to prayer in all kinds of situations. It is always inspiring and heart lifting to hear how God miraculously answered a prayer. Reflecting on answered prayer in the past, both yours and others', serves to build our current faith in God and encourages us to pray more. Share your answers to prayer with others. It will glorify God and encourage them.

Throughout the Bible, God tells His children to cry out to Him and He will hear and answer. In Jeremiah 33:3 it is written, "Call unto me, and I will answer thee, and shew thee great and mighty things, which thou knowest not." The Lord Jesus, Himself, said "Pray to thy Father which is in secret; and thy Father which seeth in secret shall reward thee openly" (Matthew 6:6).

Perhaps you are reading this today with a heavy heart. Maybe you need to be delivered from some seemingly impossible situation. Whatever your need, God has the answer. If He sees fit to not deliver you, ask and He will give you His grace and peace in your situation. The same God who delivered David three thousand years ago is the same God today. Go to Him with your situation and watch Him work on your behalf.

Thoughts on Psalm 56: Perhaps you are reading this while you feel exhausted. Perhaps you are sleep deprived and maybe even afraid. Maybe you are grieving. David in this psalm addressed all these issues.

David cried out to God. He needed the power of God to crush his enemies. David praised God's Word; he knew he could trust what God told him. Because he had God on his side, David did not fear man, who is made of flesh.

Verse 8 is particularly comforting and precious. David wrote, "Thou tellest my wanderings: put thou my tears into thy bottle: are they not in thy book?" God has a book, and in it He records facts about us. Take comfort because our tears and our wanderings are all written in God's book.

David ended this psalm with the knowledge that since God had kept him alive, He would direct him so he would be able to serve Him. God will help you with whatever you are facing today so you may better serve and glorify Him.

Prayer

Dear heavenly Father, you know I need You. You know the seemingly impossible situation in which I find myself, even at this moment. You can change the hearts of kings, so I pray You will hear and answer my humble prayers. You delivered David and so many others. I trust You will help me, because no one else can. Thank You for Your answer of peace. I pray this in Christ's name.

— —

Day 17
David Recovers All

Daily Bible Reading: 1 Samuel 30 and Psalm 27

Today's Verse: "David was greatly distressed; for the people spake of stoning him, because the soul of all the people was grieved, every man for his sons and for his daughters: but David encouraged himself in the Lord his God." (1 Samuel 30:6)

Bible Lesson: After David and his men were dismissed from the Philistine army, they returned home—a three-day journey—just to find that the city they lived in, Ziklag, had been burned and their families taken captive by the Amalekites. The men were greatly grieved, and they cried until they were cried out. The general consensus among David's followers was that this was David's fault, and they wanted to stone him to death. The Bible says David was "greatly distressed" (v. 6).

However, in the same verse is the little word "but."

"*But* David encouraged himself in the Lord his God." At this point David had no home, few loyal followers, and no family; but he still had his God. David had both the power and might of the strong Creator God and His friendship. David had what he needed, and after allowing himself a time of grieving, he had to go to war against the enemy. He inquired of the Lord and received both permission and confirmation that if he went after the Amalekites, he would be successful in recovering all the enemy had taken.

David and his six hundred men went off to battle; but after some time, two hundred of them were very tired and faint and would be of no use in fighting. David left them to guard "the stuff," and he and the other four hundred went to fight the Amalekites. Later, with the help of a forsaken servant of the Amalekites, David got some needed information. When they came to the enemy's camp, David, himself, fought for almost twenty-four hours straight, and just like God had promised, David and his men recovered all the enemy had taken.

Returning in triumph, David joined up with the two hundred men who had stayed behind, and in an unusual move, he rewarded his "reserve troops" the same way as the ones who had actively fought.

Ponderings of a Woman after God's Heart: Just because God has blessed us with something doesn't mean we don't have to sometimes fight to keep it. At times you may be on the front lines like David, while at other times you might stay by "the stuff." Either way, you are involved in a war. Here are some examples of front line fighting for what God has given you:

When you do all you can as a God-fearing wife in order to preserve your marriage, you are fighting for your marriage.

When you raise your children to love and serve God, you are fighting for their future good and fighting for them to be assets to society, not liabilities.

When you witness to your friends and coworkers, you are fighting for their souls.

When you encourage other Christians in the Lord, you are fighting against the devil's tactics to weaken them and make them useless.

Don't underestimate the power of prayer in this warfare. Praying is staying by "the stuff." It is a very powerful and vitally important action behind the scenes. Here are some examples:

- Pray for your pastor. He is on the spiritual warfare front line and needs your prayer support.

- Pray for the salvation of your unsaved loved ones.

- Pray for your country. God commands us to pray for kings and for all in authority (1 Timothy 2:2).

Your prayers are an important and vital part of a daily spiritual battle. Like David did, God will reward those who stay back with the baggage train as much as those who are on the front lines. Be a good solider for Christ today, whether on the spiritual front lines or as part of a support troop.

Thoughts on Psalm 27: In 1 Samuel 30:6 is the interesting piece of Scripture, "David encouraged himself in the Lord his God." Exactly what David said to encourage himself is not known, but he could have written or prayed something similar to this psalm.

Psalm 27 is a confident, uplifting, and precious psalm, quite fitting for anyone who needs to encourage him or herself in the Lord. This psalm begins with the strength of David's faith in his God. He got this faith because of his communion with God in His house. Faith in God and in the house of God are always connected: "So then faith cometh by hearing and hearing by the Word of God" (Romans 10:17).

David ended this psalm with the instruction to "wait on the Lord" (v. 14) and explained why—because God will strengthen your heart. And since we are impatient people, David repeated the command to simply wait on the Lord.

May this psalm bring you great comfort in your trials as you, too, wait on the Lord and receive His strength in your heart and life.

Prayer

Dear heavenly Father, help me to be a good Christian soldier. I know that in this world, according to Ephesians 6:12, we are wrestling against principalities, against powers, against the rulers of the darkness of this world, and against spiritual wickedness in high places. Please give me the strength and wisdom every day to be a good solider, since I know I am on the winning side. I ask this in the name of the risen Son of God.

— —

Day 18
Israel's Civil War

Daily Bible Reading: 2 Samuel 3 and Psalm 28

Today's Verse: "There was long war between the house of Saul and the house of David: but David waxed stronger and stronger, and the house of Saul waxed weaker and weaker." (2 Samuel 3:1)

Bible Lesson: After Saul's tragic death David became king in Hebron, but he had rule over only one of the twelve tribes of Israel, the tribe of Judah. Saul's son Ishbosheth reigned over most of the nation, comprised of the other eleven tribes. There began a civil war between the house of Saul, led by Abner, and David's supporters. All this time, Abner continued to fight for the house of Saul until he had a falling out with Ishbosheth over one of Saul's concubines. When one of the king's subordinates wanted the wife of the king, even if the king was dead, such a move was viewed as an attempt to usurp the reigning king. Ishbosheth interpreted Abner's interest in this woman as a real threat to his position. Abner then decided to change his loyalty toward David and away from Saul's son. David accepted Abner's help very graciously.

Despite the fact that David had several wives and children, David requested from Ishbosheth that he give back his first wife, Michal, Saul's daughter. Ishbosheth had no qualms about breaking up his sister's marriage and took her from her husband. Her loyal husband followed her weeping until Abner told him to go back to his now empty house.

Abner, in his new position as leader over David's men, immediately showed his leadership skills and took charge, intending to bring all of Ishbosheth's people under David's rule and to unite Israel. When Joab, one of David's men and also his nephew, heard about Abner's new position in David's kingdom, he was not pleased and believed Abner might possibly be a traitor. Joab hated Abner since Abner had killed Joab's brother Asahel in their last battle. Joab then murdered Abner.

When King David heard about the death of Abner, he wept bitterly. He surely remembered his promise to Saul that when he became king, he would not kill Saul's house, and Abner was Saul's uncle (1 Samuel 14:50).

In touching grief, David ordered all of Israel to mourn the death of Abner, calling him a "prince and a great man" (2 Samuel 3:38). The needless murder by David's nephew Joab was a great grief to the heart of David.

With David's mourning of Abner, the people realized it was not the will of their new king to kill this man. The people of Israel loved David, and "whatsoever the king did pleased all the people" (v. 36).

Ponderings of a Woman after God's Heart: The struggle between the house of David and the house of Saul that went on for years is an example of the struggle between the flesh and the spirit of God in our lives. David had God's blessing, and he was divinely ordained to be king of Israel, yet this position did not come without struggle and opposition from the house of the former king.

After we are saved, there is a struggle because our flesh wants to serve its sinful self. Galatians 5:17 puts it this way, "For the flesh lusteth against the Spirit, and the Spirit against the flesh: and these are contrary the one to the other: so that ye cannot do the things that ye would." The believer still has to battle the flesh in God's will in order to serve God. This long war may only end when he or she is in heaven.

You may have a pet sin you struggle with daily. Good! Yes, you read that right. I am applauding you because if you struggle, you have not given in totally. You are like the house of David. You are gaining strength daily as you commit your desire to change to the Lord. As you grow in grace and in the knowledge of our Lord and Savior Jesus Christ daily, the hold of sin on you gets weaker and weaker because you become spiritually stronger.

Thoughts on Psalm 28: This psalm was probably written after David became king of Israel. Initially, he was king of a divided nation and had enemies. David knew who to go to for help—God. It seemed the enemies of King David were those who were enemies of his God too.

Verse 5 is an interesting statement made by David: "Because they regard not the works of the Lord, nor the operation of his hands, he shall destroy them, and not build them up." God built up David's kingdom because David trusted in Him. Contrariwise, God allowed Ishbosheth to be destroyed. Perhaps part of the reason Ishbosheth was destroyed was because he did not regard the works of the Lord.

David went on to end this psalm with thanks to God. Because David trusted in God, all his people benefited. The God-fearing leader wanted God's blessing not only for himself but also for all of his subjects. He desired that all of his people would be protected, saved, fed, and upheld by God.

Thank God today for the God-fearing leaders you know, whether they are in your home or church or in secular leadership. Pray God will help and strengthen them as they seek God's help also.

Prayer

Dear heavenly Father, I come to you weakened by all of my sinful desires. Please help me to become spiritually strong so I can serve You far better. I need Your help, especially in (name the area you struggle with). I thank You in advance for giving me the victory. I ask this in the name of the One who was victorious over death. Amen.

– –

Day 19
The Death of Ishbosheth

Daily Bible Reading: 2 Samuel 4 and Psalm 35

Today's Verse: "How much more, when wicked men have slain a righteous person in his own house upon his bed? shall I not therefore now require his blood of your hand, and take you away from the earth?" (2 Samuel 4:11)

Bible Lesson: I am sure David wanted to peacefully unite all of Israel's tribes under his rule. He was the king chosen by God, yet most of the nation of Israel followed Saul's son Ishbosheth. Ishbosheth obviously depended very heavily upon Abner's leadership, and after Abner was murdered by Joab, King Ishbosheth became very discouraged and depressed.

Some of Ishbosheth's people surmised that they would soon be ruled over by David because they knew Ishbosheth was a weak and beaten leader, and the only other relative left to inherit the throne of Saul's kingdom was his lame grandson, Mephibosheth. His physical infirmities made him unfit not only for the role of king but also for his inability to avenge the murder of his uncle Abner.

The brothers Baanah and Rechab, both captains in Saul's army, were opportunists. They decided to eliminate their king and bring the great news to David in hopes of a great reward and position of honor in David's kingdom. Rechab and Baanah went to Ishbosheth at noon under false pretenses, where he was sleeping in his bed, and stabbed him under his fifth rib. This area of the body ensures a quick death because the heart is between the fifth and sixth ribs. After they stabbed him, they removed his head and took it to King David in Hebron, thinking they had done a great deed for David. They were expecting a reward. David was enraged. These wicked men had killed an innocent man, their king, in what should have been his place of extreme safety—his own house—while at rest in his own bed. Their actions showed the wickedest treachery.

King David's behavior, upon hearing the news, showed both his integrity and virtue. Although the kingdom of Saul was then secure with Ishbosheth gone, David displayed his abhorrence of their treachery and immediately executed justice by putting them to death. He publicly announced his utter detestation of their deed and cut off their hands and feet—the bodily members that were used in this terrible act—and hanged them as a testimony against them. David's public actions announced to his kingdom that he would not be served by treachery and murder, nor would he condone such deeds. David then proceeded to honorably bury the head of Ishbosheth in the sepulcher of Abner.

Ponderings of a Woman after God's Heart: David never rejoiced upon learning of Ishbosheth's death. Proverbs 24:17-18 reads, "Rejoice not when thine enemy falleth, and let not thine heart be glad when he stumbleth: lest the Lord see it, and it displease him, and he turn away his wrath from him."

You probably have some people in your life you don't like. You may even consider them your enemies. When you hear of bad things happening to them, it may be hard to be like David and refrain from rejoicing. This verse in Proverbs is a hard one to practice since—let's admit it—our flesh likes to see our enemies suffer. However, God sees our heart, and when He sees our pleasure at His judgment on the guilty ones, we bring God's displeasure upon us, "for the wrath of man worketh not the righteousness of God" (James 1:20). I also believe the righteous judgments of God are not intended to satisfy our wrath on our enemies. When we see calamity of any sort strike those we don't like, it is not for us to rejoice. We should carefully consider our lives instead because the same God who is displeased with the actions of our enemies may be displeased with some of the things we do.

Thoughts on Psalm 35: It is not known under what circumstances David penned this particular psalm, but verses 13 and 14 are very fitting in how David behaved at the death of his rival Ishbosheth, Saul's son and king of the greater part of Israel. In these verses, David described how he mourned and grieved when those who slandered him were sick.

David's actions in this psalm are similar to the words of Jesus, "I say unto you, love your enemies, bless them that curse you, do good to them that hate you, and pray for them which despitefully use you and persecute you" (Matthew 5:44).

It is indeed the mark of a true child of God to care for those who have wronged them. God has promised to take vengeance upon the evildoers. Nevertheless, the children of God must show God's love and kindness to those who have done them wrong.

Prayer

Dear heavenly Father, please forgive me for the many times I was secretly happy to hear of the misfortunes of those I did not like. Help me rather to sincerely weep with those who weep, no matter how much I dislike them. Please help me to live sincerely before You so You will be pleased with all of my thoughts, words, and deeds, and please help me to not do anything to incur Your righteous displeasure on me. I humbly ask this in the name of Jesus Christ.

- -

Day 20
David's Third and Final Anointing as King

Daily Bible Reading: 2 Samuel 5 and Psalm 92

Today's Verse: "All the elders of Israel came to the King to Hebron; and King David made a league with them in Hebron before the Lord: and they anointed David king over Israel." (2 Samuel 5:3)

Bible Lesson: In this chapter, David was anointed king of Israel for the third time in his life. At thirty years of age, he was finally king over the entire nation of Israel. The first thing he did in his new office was take the city of Jerusalem from the Jebusites who inhabited it.

The Jebusites were confident David could not come into their city because of the "blind and the lame" (v. 6). "The blind and the lame were hated of David's soul" (v. 8). This is not referring to handicapped people but to the idols of the Jebusites. The Jebusites were trusting in their helpless idols to protect them from any invasion.

Jerusalem's name means "vision of peace," and it is a very important biblical city. Joab conquered the city in the king's name, and David made it the capital of Israel (1 Chronicles 11:6). After settling in Jerusalem, Hiram, king of Tyre, who was no doubt a believer in the one true God also, graciously provided David the materials to build himself a house there.

While in Jerusalem, David took several wives and concubines for himself. One estimate is he fathered a total of nineteen sons. While polygamy was common with oriental kings, David went against God's law—God expressly forbade the kings of Israel to have multiple wives (Deuteronomy 17:17).

While David was establishing his new government with the blessing of God, he still had challenges. Soon after he became king, the Philistine army came, seeking to destroy David. David knew he had to fight them, yet before he did anything, he first inquired of God, asking Him two specific questions about the upcoming battle: Shall I go up? and Will You deliver them? God's answer to both of David's questions was yes.

After this success, the Philistines again challenged David. Again, David asked counsel of the Lord, this time receiving a different battle strategy. David followed God's orders and defeated the Philistines a second time.

Ponderings of a Woman after God's Heart: Sometimes the blessings of God take some time. Although David was promised the kingdom at a very young age, it was not until he was thirty years old that this was fully realized. Let me encourage you to wait on God's timing, no matter where in life you find yourself.

King David was humble enough to know that the same God who made him king would also help him rule Israel. He asked God for His direction and His help in conquering both the Jebusites and the Philistines. Although wars were normal on the king's daily to-do list, he depended on God for His help and advice. This was true when he conquered Jerusalem from the Jebusites. The fact that he destroyed the useless idols was evidence of his dependence on the one true and living God. Then he went on to fight the Philistines. Although he'd had success against the Philistines before, David did not go into battle without first getting specific direction from God.

Seek the mind of God in all of your daily decisions. Perhaps you were successful in the past and now, without seeking God's help, you forge ahead. Just like David, God's direction may not be one size fits all; it may change with time and circumstances. Ask for His guidance and then seek to glorify Him in all of your decisions.

Thoughts on Psalm 143: After pleading for the Lord to hear and help him, David asked for God's direction specifically "in the morning" (v. 8). David was asking God to direct him in his decisions throughout the day. This is a good plan of action for all of us. Let me encourage you to seek God first thing in the morning and invite Him to be with you the entire day so He can guide you in all of your daily decisions.

David then asked God to teach him His will (v. 10). David wanted to do God's will for his life. David knew and showed us in this psalm that asking for and following God's direction would lead him to blessing.

This psalm is a bit similar to the words of Solomon, King David's son, who later wrote, "Trust in the Lord with all thine heart; and lean not unto thine own understanding" (Proverbs 3:5). Sometimes a decision may be obvious to you, but instead of trusting your own understanding of the situation, ask God for His mind and follow His guidance to be led in the way of blessing.

Prayer

Dear heavenly Father, help me to know what You desire me to do. Whatever Your will is for me, please help me to do it. I ask that You will help me remember to always ask You for direction in all of my decisions and then depend upon You in all of my daily tasks. Help me to not be prideful of my past accomplishments but rather to remember that all I am and all I may accomplish is only because of You and only for Your glory, praise, and honor. I humbly ask this in the name of Your precious Son, Christ Jesus.

- -

Day 21
David Does a Good Thing the Right Way

Daily Bible Reading: 1 Chronicles 15 and Psalm 96

Today's Verse: "David said, None ought to carry the ark of God but the Levites: for them hath the Lord chosen to carry the ark of God, and to minister unto him for ever." (1 Chronicles 15:2)

Bible Lesson: Many years ago, God told Moses to build the tabernacle and put the ark of the covenant inside it. This wooden box overlaid with gold was the physical dwelling place of Jehovah God. All during the Israelites' wanderings in the wilderness, their entrance into the promised land, and their lives through all of the times of the judges and during the reign of Saul, the tabernacle housed the ark.

After David settled in Jerusalem, he wanted the presence of his God near him, so he made plans to bring the ark of God to him using a brand-new cart to carry it. However, God had specifically told Moses that certain of the priestly tribe of Levi were only to carry the ark on their shoulders, as it was never to be touched directly (Numbers 7:9). During the transport the oxen stumbled, and a priest named Uzzah grabbed the ark to steady it, whereupon God immediately struck him dead. David, fearing God's wrath, placed the ark in the house of Obed-edom for three months.

David was determined to bring the ark from the house of Obed-edom, and this time he did it God's way. As you read 1 Chronicles 15, you find many names mentioned. The Holy Spirit took special care to single out these men who had this important task. They were real people with a special job, and they did an honorable work. Their memorial is having their names recorded in holy writ.

The procession of the ark of God, carried on the shoulders of the sons of Kohath, was accompanied with great joy, much music, praises to God, singing, dancing, and sacrifices. God blessed this joyous celebration, and the ark was placed in a tent David had prepared for it in Jerusalem.

Ponderings of a Woman after God's Heart: God commanded His people to not forsake "the assembling of ourselves together" (Hebrews 10:25). In today's world of technology, some Christians substitute TV or internet preaching, as good as it may be, for actual attendance at a local church. This is doing a good thing the wrong way. Faithfully attending a local, physical church is doing things God's way. Here are some of the many blessings for obeying God by being a part of a local church:

You have people to pray for you. (Along with my church's prayer meeting and our prayer chain, the people of my church do a lot of praying for those of our church family.)

You have a pastor who will visit you when you are in the hospital. (Your favorite TV/internet preacher probably won't come to the hospital to pray with you when you are sick.)

You have people who will help you when you are in need. (I have both been helped and helped out those in my church family many times.)

You have access to godly men and women who will answer your Bible questions.

If you are single, church is a great way to meet your spouse. (I know because I did!)

You have access to free godly counsel when you need it. (Again, the TV preacher may very well be a no-show.)

You have a place to invite your unsaved friends to hear the gospel and be led to the Lord. (Many souls have been saved through the ministry of my church.)

God told you to assemble with other believers; therefore, He expects you to do so and He has provided a church home for you. It will not be perfect, I guarantee, but there is a church for you. If you have not yet found it, ask God to guide you until you are where He wants you to be.

Thoughts on Psalm 96: This psalm was composed when David brought the ark of the covenant to Jerusalem. The psalm starts out telling everyone—both the nation of Israel and all of the gentiles—to praise the Lord (vv. 1–3). God alone is worthy to be praised since He is the Creator. Although the heathens are religious and have their gods, their gods can do neither good nor evil. The Lord is the Creator of the universe, and as Creator, He alone deserves to be worshiped.

This psalm is prophetic, looking forward to Christ's coming kingdom on earth when He will judge all nations. Verse 10 instructs us to tell the heathen (non-Jew) "the Lord reigneth."

Verses 11–13 relate how the entire realm of nature rejoices when these glories will occur. Christ, the Creator of all nature, will rule over His works in righteousness and will judge with truth. Since there will be such rejoicing when Christ reigns over the entire earth in the future, let Him rule in your heart and life now to experience just a bit of heaven on this imperfect earth.

Prayer

Dear heavenly Father, thank You for loving me so much that You have provided the organization of a local church. Help me to serve You by faithfully attending and serving in my church. Bless all that are a part of my church, and help us to work together for Your glory so precious, lost souls will be saved. In Jesus's name, amen.

--

Day 22
When God Says No

Daily Bible Reading: 2 Samuel 7 and Psalm 92

Today's Verse: "Let thy name be magnified for ever, saying, The Lord of hosts is the God over Israel: and let the house of thy servant David be established before thee." (2 Samuel 7:26)

Bible Lesson: David was finally established as king over the entire united nation of Israel. He was about thirty-seven years old at that time and had settled into his house in Jerusalem. Then he wanted to build a house for God. He felt guilty that although he had a house, the ark of God—the dwelling place of Jehovah—resided "within curtains" (v. 2).

David shared his desire to build a temple for the Lord with the prophet Nathan. Nathan agreed with King David and told him to go ahead with his plans because it sounded like an excellent idea. That night, Nathan had a vision from God, and God gave him a message to take back to David. In short, the message was that David would not build God a house, but his son would. God went on to tell Nathan He would establish David's throne forever.

After Nathan delivered this message to David, the king sat before the Lord and talked. He was disappointed God denied him his desire to build Him a house, but he was both humbled and grateful God promised to make David's kingdom one that would last forever. Unlike Saul, who could not pass his kingdom to his sons, David's dynasty would continue forever.

David's descendancy to both Mary—the biological mother of Jesus, and Joseph—the foster father of Jesus, can be traced all the way to Jesus Christ "the Son of David." David's kingly rule would continue through to Jesus Christ, when He will rule the world from Jerusalem for one thousand years. This is prophesied by Isaiah: "Of the increase of his government and peace there shall be no end, upon the throne of David, and upon his kingdom, to order it, and to establish it with judgment and with justice from henceforth even forever" (Isaiah 9:7).

Ponderings of a Woman after God's Heart: When David got the message from God through Nathan and went and talked with God, I am sure he had mixed feelings. He was disappointed it would not be himself but his son who would build God's house. God tempered David's disappointment when He promised David, "I will build thee a house" (v. 27).

When you have disappointments in your life, even when you have a good and noble desire, and God says no, let David be an example for you. Go to God and talk to Him about it; accept His will for you. Don't fuss and pout but instead ask God to give you a glimpse of His greater plan for you. He has your best interests at heart and knows far more than you do. God is probably planning something better for you, even something better for eternity, which you don't—or even cannot—understand right now.

Talk to God about your disappointments, even when you are disappointed with Him. Ask Him for an answer of peace that will calm and comfort your heart. Remember that this life is not everything. Eternity is ahead, and sometimes what is denied in this life may be saved for later, something that will bless us for all eternity.

Perhaps some of the joys denied for us in this life may be given back to us in an eternal form in heaven as part of the blessings and rewards from our Lord and Savior. Trust in the Lord; He sees the big picture when we cannot. When we are denied something that may be very dear to us, God may have something far greater in mind that we cannot imagine now. Trust Him to do right for you; He always will.

Thoughts on Psalm 92: David wrote this psalm even though it is not attributed to him. The introduction says this is a psalm for the Sabbath day. This psalm of thanks and praise is appropriate at a time of rest and reflection on the great goodness and faithfulness of the Lord.

The curious phrase "on an instrument of ten strings" (v. 3) is found three times in the book of Psalms. This may not actually be a reference to a musical instrument but rather to the human body. David was saying he would use all of himself to give thanks and praise to God.

The psalm goes on with David's meditation of God's goodness to him. David said, "I shall be anointed with fresh oil" (v.10). This is most likely David's reference to his third and final anointing as king—when he became king over the entire nation of Israel.

With supreme confidence, and no doubt looking ahead to his own advancing years, David said the righteous ones will flourish. Those planted in the house of the Lord will, despite their elderliness, be fruitful. To bear spiritual fruit, despite chronological age, is a wonderful promise and comfort that God's servants are valued and useful in their service for Him, even in old age.

Prayer

Dear heavenly Father, please help me to talk to You in times of disappointment. When You deny my requests here, help me to realize You truly are in control and only will do what is best for me. Help me to trust in You and in Your will for me. Help me to live daily laying up heavenly and eternal rewards. Let me lay up in heaven what I cannot keep on earth. I ask this in the name of the Messiah, amen.

– –

Day 23
David and Mephibosheth

Daily Bible Reading: 2 Samuel 9 and Psalm 145

Today's Verse: "Mephibosheth dwelt in Jerusalem: for he did eat continually at the king's table; and was lame on both his feet." (2 Samuel 9:13)

Bible Lesson: During his first several years as king over the united nation of Israel, David had many political duties to attend to, including fighting several wars with the ancient enemies of Israel. After he successfully captured their lands and cities, he then turned his attention homeward.

Years before, Jonathan had specifically asked David to show kindness to his children after God had established David's kingdom. David needed to fulfill his promise toward his friend, so he requested a search be made to find any relatives of Saul in order to show them kindness.

A servant of Saul's was found who informed King David that Jonathan had a son named Mephibosheth whose feet were lame. Most likely Mephibosheth was just a baby when Jonathan requested kindness from David, because 2 Samuel 4:4 reads that at the time of Jonathan's death, Mephibosheth was five years old. Mephibosheth was hiding in Lodebar. Lodebar means "no pasture, no hope, desolation." The crippled Mephibosheth went from being a young child to becoming a father himself in this place of fear and hiding. Crippled, exiled from home, and without hope, he received the summons from the new king one day.

Royal messengers were sent to escort Mephibosheth to the court of King David. He went, quite possibly in fear and trembling, only to find his supposedly erstwhile enemy was his father's best friend. King David's first words to this frightened young man were "fear not" (2 Samuel 9:7). David made sure the crippled Mephibosheth was to be treated as a valued member of the royal household and was to eat daily at the king's table as one of the king's sons. David all but adopted this son of Jonathan as his own.

Ponderings of a Woman after God's Heart: This is a beautiful story with wonderful meanings. We come to God for salvation as sinful human beings. We are totally helpless, just as Mephibosheth was—lame in both his feet, yet God takes us and makes us His sons and daughters, inviting us to dine at His table continually.

Then, as Christians, sometimes we return to Lodebar. We find ourselves in the place of no hope, no pasture, and utter desolation.

Do you ever find yourself so discouraged and despondent with life in general that you feel there is no hope? Instead of looking brighter, tomorrow threatens to be as dreary as today—if not worse. You pray and cry out to God, yet it seems He is not listening; you seem to get no answer from heaven. If this is you, you are living in Lodebar. However, this is no place for you to stay. Instead, cry out to God for help and expect the help you need will come. He wants to pluck you from the depths of Lodebar and place you at His table—with all of your needs supplied and His very presence to cheer and to guide you.

Here are some tips to get you out of Lodebar:

- **Confess**—Confess any and all of your sins to God including the sin of unbelief that He does not care for you. If you say He does not care, you are calling Him a liar.

- **Pray**—Ask God for His guidance and expect to get it.

- **Read**—Read the Bible. Psalms is a good place to start when you are feeling despair.

- **Fellowship**—Make sure you go to church. Just being around other Christians will lift your spirits, and you can ask them to pray for you. You can be as specific or as nonspecific as you want.

- **Talk**—Sometimes you need godly counsel. Do what you can to get the guidance you need.

Thoughts on Psalm 145: Although this psalm was written by David, the sentiments expressed could very well have been those of Mephibosheth, and they should be those of every believer in Christ. This beautiful song of praise aptly expresses so many of the wonderful works of God, even to those who do not acknowledge Him.

In this psalm, David called for the entire creation to praise the Lord. He alone is worthy of this praise, not only because He is the Creator but because of the care He gives to all of His creation.

This psalm ends with the beautiful verse "My mouth shall speak the praise of the Lord: and let all flesh bless his holy name for ever and ever" (v. 21). The phrase "all flesh" seems to include the animal kingdom too. What a beautiful thought—that even the animals praise their Creator. And why shouldn't they? The animal kingdom may in some cases give God more glory than their more intelligent human counterparts.

Prayer

Dear heavenly Father, thank You for this touching account of Mephibosheth. When I feel totally helpless like him, help me to realize You are my only help and You can and will lift me up. Help me to turn to You and trust in You as You help me live a victorious Christian life every day. I ask this all in Christ's name, amen.

— —

Day 24
David's Affair with Bathsheba

Daily Bible Reading: 2 Samuel 11 and Psalm 6

Today's Verse: "The thing that David had done displeased the Lord." (2 Samuel 11:27)

Bible Lesson: Chapter 11 of 2 Samuel records one of the most infamous acts of David—his affair with Bathsheba, the wife of Uriah the Hittite, one of David's mighty men.

At this point in his life, David was likely a middle-aged man. Regardless, it appears from the text he was suffering from what we call today a midlife crisis.

In our Bible text, he sent Joab and all of the army of Israel to battle to destroy the Ammonites and take the city of Rabbah. But for whatever reason, David did not go to battle with his army; instead, he remained at home in Jerusalem. One night he couldn't sleep, and looking out of his window, he saw the lovely Bathsheba bathing herself a short distance away. Stirred, he decided a romantic evening with her would be the perfect cure for his insomnia. He followed through on his decision, one thing led to another, and a few weeks later Bathsheba sent David a message telling him he was going to be a father.

In desperation, David tried to cover up his sin. He summoned Uriah to him under the pretense of getting news from the front. Then he sent Uriah home to be with his wife to shift the blame off of himself, but David's plan didn't work. The noble Uriah refused to enjoy the comforts of home and the love of his wife, saying his master Joab and all of the other soldiers were roughing it, so why should he be in comfort and enjoyment when they were not? Uriah stayed and slept in the servants' quarters in the palace. David tried again the next day to send Uriah home, but he still refused out of loyalty to his fellow soldiers and his king.

David, realizing his plan was not working, then sent Uriah back to the battlefield with a note to Joab instructing him to place Uriah at the most dangerous place of battle and leave him there. David specifically told Joab to retreat; the plan was to keep Joab safe but have Uriah killed. This strategy worked and Uriah perished in battle.

Joab sent a messenger back to David with the news of the battle, telling him all that happened and specifically, that Uriah the Hittite was killed. David sent back the message with tips to overthrow the city and told Joab "the sword devoureth one as well as another" (2 Samuel 11:25). These last words, although addressed to Joab concerning Uriah, were more to assuage David's guilty conscience than to inform Joab of the obvious.

Bathsheba was now a widow. When the news of her husband's death came to her, she mourned for her husband. Surely she must have connected her husband's death with the king's baby, which she was carrying. She must have felt heartbreaking grief because of the loss of her husband, anger at David for killing her husband, and mixed feelings toward her unborn child.

David thought he had successfully pulled off the whole nasty affair. He soon married the widowed Bathsheba and she gave him a son, another prince, but the chapter ends with the ominous words, "But the thing that David had done displeased the Lord" (v. 27). God had seen everything and He was not happy.

Ponderings of a Woman after God's Heart: The lesson we should learn from this sad series of events in David's life is that God sees all. David thought he had gotten away with his fling with Bathsheba. It seemed he did at first, but as Moses told the children of Israel hundreds of years earlier, when they sinned against the Lord, they were to be sure their sin would find them out (Numbers 32:23).

Actions both good and evil, done in the dark and in secret, are no match for an all-seeing God. The entire series of events (recorded in 2 Samuel 11) covers the space of at least nine months. All of that time,

David went about his daily kingly activities carrying his guilty secret. He was like Adam who, after he sinned, hid himself from God because he was afraid. David did wrong, but he did not want to go to God and repent.

Thoughts on Psalm 6: This is a psalm of confession to the Lord. David may have written this psalm after his transgression with Bathsheba. He knew he had sinned against God, and he cried out to the Lord for His mercy. David knew his sin needed to be addressed by God and David submitted to this, but he pleaded that God would not do so in His anger or His hot displeasure, knowing God's righteous wrath would destroy him totally.

David was physically ill at this point. Perhaps this is because of his great, soul-wrenching grief over his sin and its effect—even on his enemies. The reference to David's enemies may be in connection with the prophet Nathan's words, "By this deed thou hast given great occasion to the enemies of the Lord to blaspheme" (2 Samuel 12:14).

David, by example, leads the sinful ones to cleansing confession to the Savior, who not only will hear our prayers but who is also faithful and just to forgive us our sins and to cleanse us from all unrighteousness.

Prayer

Dear heavenly Father, please help me daily to realize You do see all things. Please give me the wisdom to do the right things when I am tempted to sin. When I do sin, please help me to come and repent to You, knowing You are faithful and just to forgive my sins. Help me in secret to do right rather than evil, knowing You do see in secret. I ask this in my Savior's name, amen.

— —

Day 25
The Fallout of David's Affair

Daily Bible Reading: 2 Samuel 12 and Psalm 51

Today's Verse: "Nathan said to David, Thou art the man." (2 Samuel 12:7)

Bible Lesson: Nathan—the same prophet who years earlier communicated with David about the possibility of building God's temple—was sent to David to convey God's displeasure of his secret sin.

Nathan told King David a fictitious story about two men, one rich and one poor. All the poor man had was a precious little ewe lamb he treated like a daughter. The rich man had flocks and herds; yet, when the rich man needed meat, instead of killing one of his own animals, he took, killed, and ate the poor man's pet lamb.

David was incensed at this man who did such a cruel and heartless act. He swiftly and angrily pronounced a twofold judgment on the man:

The man was to restore the lamb fourfold, as it was commanded in the law of Moses (Leviticus 22:1).

The man was to die.

Then Nathan uttered the telling and haunting words: "Thou art the man." The story was fiction but the facts were not.

David's face probably crumpled before he started to weep bitterly, as he realized God knew what he had done. David may have been fearing for his own life since part of the judgment he ordered on the fictitious man was that he was to die. Nathan told David that he, the king, killed Uriah the Hittite using the sword of the Amorites and then took Uriah's wife. He further said that David despised God. Although God would have mercy on David's life and he would not die, his punishment would include the following:

The sword would not depart from his house, and

four of his sons, including Bathsheba's newborn baby boy, would die.

Nathan went on to tell David that by his foolish deeds, David gave the Lord's enemies reason to blaspheme because he was a very poor testimony of a godly man.

Soon after Nathan left, David and Bathsheba's baby got very sick. David fasted and prayed that God would heal the baby and let him live, but after seven days the baby died.

David's servants were afraid to tell him his baby had died., yet David surprised them by first worshiping God and then eating. When they wondered at David's peace now his baby had died, David told them these wonderful words: "I shall go to him, but he shall not return to me" (2 Samuel 12:23).

In the course of a year, Bathsheba had lost her first husband and her firstborn child. Although both were his fault, David comforted his wife and she conceived again. This son was named Solomon, meaning "peaceable," and it is recorded that "the Lord loved him" (v. 24). Nathan the prophet called him Jedidiah, meaning, "the beloved of the Lord" (v. 25). Solomon succeeded David on the throne.

Ponderings of a Woman after God's Heart: The wonderful truth that comes out of this sad story is the promise that innocent children go straight to heaven when they die. David's baby, although born in sin, was an innocent being. David worshiped God even in this terrible time, knowing someday he, too, would die and go to paradise, where he would be reunited forever with his son.

The words of David during this sad time are a comfort for anyone who has lost a child either through miscarriage, illness, stillbirth, or even abortion. Heaven welcomes these precious, tiny souls. As sad as it is when a baby loses its life—never to know the joys of riding a bicycle, having a pet, or falling in love—this child has the fullness of heaven to enjoy. The same little one who was denied the joys of growing up on earth will never experience the pain of falling off a bike, losing a beloved pet, or having its heart broken. Infants taken to heaven experience more joy than we can ever know in our mortal bodies.

Thoughts on Psalm 51: This is an anguished cry from a sinful human being as he sees the effects of sin in his life. Written by David after Nathan approached him about his sin with Bathsheba, David cried out to God for His mercy.

David was not making excuses for himself rather acknowledging his original and deplorable sinful nature (v. 5). He realized a sinful being such as himself must take great care to be even more righteous before God. He cried out not only to be forgiven but to also be restored to God's favor and to enjoy again the wonderful feelings that accompany close communication with God.

David promised that with God's restoring power, he would teach others the ways of God. The last two verses seem to be King David's plea that his personal sin, now made public, would not further hurt God's people. This soul-touching psalm of David teaches us today at least two important facts about the gravity of private sin:

1. It will be made known and
2. it will hurt others.

Prayer

Dear heavenly Father, I am so thankful that You take such good care of small children. We know those who have been taken from us in death are with You. They brought us many moments of joy, and so many tears after they were gone, but we are comforted in knowing You have them. You love and protect these little ones far better than we ever could. Thank You for Your tender care. I thank Thee in the name of Your Son who conquered death and the grave, amen.

-- --

Day 26
Absalom's Revolt

Daily Bible Reading: 2 Samuel 15 and Psalm 3

Today's Verse: "It came to pass, that when David was come to the top of the mount, where he worshiped God, behold, Hushai the Archite came to meet him with his coat rent, and earth upon his head." (2 Samuel 15:32)

Bible Lesson: David reaped the consequences of his having committed adultery and murder. As the prophet Nathan had said, "The sword will never depart from thy house" (2 Samuel 12:10). David's firstborn son, Amnon, raped his sister Tamar, who was very close to her brother Absalom (2 Samuel 13). Two years later, Absalom murdered Amnon. Amnon was the second son of David to die young.

Absalom fled the country after he murdered his brother, but years later, at the request of Joab, David allowed Absalom to return home. Absalom then used his beauty and charm in an attempt to steal his father's kingdom (2 Samuel 15) and sent spies throughout all of Israel to let everyone know he was the reigning king.

David was probably in his sixties at this time and may not have been in good health. The people may have believed Absalom, and they were ready and willing to accept this handsome, young man as their king, even before David died. Perhaps they also thought it was the king's desire to give the kingdom to his son earlier than expected. At any rate, "the people increased continually with Absalom" (v. 12).

When David got the news Absalom was trying to take over his kingdom and that he had quite a large following, David knew he had to flee for his life. Most of his former loyal subjects were now following Absalom, including his counselor Ahithophel. Nevertheless, there were a few faithful ones who followed David from Jerusalem into the wilderness.

The aged king went up Mount Olivet barefoot and weeping with his head covered—all signs of deep distress, sorrow, and humility. At the top of Mount Olivet, David worshiped God, and immediately God sent him help in the form of Hushai the Archite, David's friend. David told the faithful Hushai to return to Jerusalem as he would be more of an asset to David there in defeating the counsel of Ahithophel, and to send a report back to King David.

Ponderings of a Woman after God's Heart: David's flight from his son Absalom and Jerusalem was not a trial like the one years earlier, when he was on the run from King Saul. This time, David was reaping what he had sown from his sin with Bathsheba. But during this crisis, David did something very unusual: when he came to the top of Mount Olivet, he worshipped God. I wonder what exactly David said to God as he took time to worship Him at this very painful point in his life.

This is the second time it's recorded in Scripture that David actively worshiped God. The first time was immediately after his son with Bathsheba died (2 Samuel 12:20). Now another son was out to murder him and seize the kingdom. In worshiping God, David was accepting his punishment, but he was also relying on God's mercy.

Worshiping God is telling God He can do what He wants with us. He is in control, He is our Creator, and we can do nothing. Worshiping God is willingly accepting His will for us, even when He allows bitter events in our lives. Worshiping God is telling God we love Him because we know He loves us. We are His, and we choose to willingly submit to Him, even when it is painful for us to do so. We also know that despite our sins and failures, He will see us through. This is true worship, and it's what David did in his times of extreme disappointment and heartbreak.

Thoughts on Psalm 3: Written at a terrible time in David's life, Psalm 3 is a very comforting portion of Scripture. Someone has aptly said that when all you have is God, God is all you need. David wrote his psalm while running for his life from his son Absalom and his followers. Being vastly outnumbered, and despite family problems, David knew the Lord had not forsaken him. This knowledge was all David needed.

Verses 4 and 5 are particularly precious under the circumstances. David said he cried to the Lord for His help. Then, knowing his prayers were heard, he went to bed and slept peacefully. He was able to sleep knowing God was protecting him through the night. The next morning, he awoke alive and intact.

David ended this psalm with the statement that he expected salvation from the Lord — not from any other source—because God would bless His people. He closed the psalm with the word "Selah," reminding the reader to pause and meditate on what he'd written.

Prayer

Dear heavenly Father, help me to remember and be like David. Even in times when I am reaping the consequences of my sin, help me to submit totally to You and to Your will for me, knowing You are ever merciful and that You will send me help even when I don't deserve Your gracious mercy. Help me to worship You because You are God and I am but Your creation. Thank You for loving me and helping me to accept Your will. I pray this in the name which is above every name, the name of Jesus Christ, amen.

— —

Day 27
Deal Gently with Absalom

Daily Bible Reading: 2 Samuel 18 and Psalm 69

Today's Verse: "The king was much moved, and went up to the chamber over the gate, and wept: and as he went, thus he said, O my son Absalom, my son, my son Absalom! would God I had died for thee, O Absalom, my son, my son!" (2 Samuel 18:33)

Bible Lesson: The rebellion of Absalom resulted in a battle, as there would not be two kings. One or the other must rule, the other die. Those following Absalom were determined to dispatch David, and David was determined to fight for his life and for his kingdom. David divided all of his loyal men into three companies, one each under Joab, Abishai, and Ittai. Before the battle commenced, David gave a special command, saying, "Deal gently for my sake with the young man, even with Absalom" (2 Samuel 18:5).

The battle began in the wooded area in Ephraim. Fighting in the wilderness proved treacherous and there were losses on each side. The total death toll was twenty thousand men.

Absalom, in trying to escape, ran into some of David's men. These men who had heard the command of the king did not dare lay a hand on the escaping usurper. Absalom's mule panicked, and while rushing through the forest, the animal ran under the boughs of an oak tree. Absalom's head became firmly wedged between the boughs, possibly so tight he began choking. One of David's men saw him hanging there and informed Joab, who told the solider he should have killed him. The soldier protested that the king's command was to "beware that none touch the young man Absalom" (v. 12). Joab blatantly ignored David's command and instead thrust three darts through the heart of Absalom while he was still alive and hanging in the tree. Then ten of Joab's men killed him.

The ignoble death of Absalom ended the war. The usurper was now dead. His body was cast into a deep pit in the woods and stones were piled upon it. A messenger was sent to King David, who was anxiously awaiting news of the battle—especially of Absalom's fate. David got the terrible news his son was dead. This chapter ends with David's tears and brokenhearted grief over the death of his much loved but rebellious son.

Ponderings of a Woman after God's Heart: It is against nature for a parent to bury a child; the death of one is every parent's greatest fear and dread. However, in this scenario of David and Absalom, David seemed to point out the even greater heartache of the loss of a child to eternal separation rather than to the glories of paradise and temporary separation. This seems to be the case with Absalom.

Most likely, any parent who has ever suffered the devastating loss of a child has the same cry as David: "Would God I had died for thee" (v. 33). Had David, with his heart for God, been killed instead of Absalom, he would have been in paradise, but only hell accepted the soul of Absalom. Unlike the death of David's infant son several years earlier, Absalom, who not only rebelled against his father but also against God, was lost to David forever.

Just as the bliss of heaven is real to us, so also should be the eternal fires of hell. Children of godly parents who have once professed salvation in Christ but are now living godless lives, perhaps even raising their own children without them hearing the message of redemption, may have never actually accepted God's great gift of salvation, like Absalom. By doing so, they are endangering their children with the possibility of a Christless eternity in hell.

Thoughts on Psalm 69: Like a drowning man, David reached for the lifeline of his God in this psalm. The psalm seems to be written in a terrible time in David's life. He wrote, "I am weary of my crying" (v. 3). Although God did not answer him swiftly, David did not lose faith.

He still waited for his God, despite being surrounded by numerous, malicious, and powerful enemies.

Do you ever feel weary of your crying? Maybe you think you are doing everything right before God. You are faithful in His house, you love His Word, you cry out to God for His help, but there is no one to pity or comfort you. Meanwhile, you may feel everyone and everything is against you.

David went on to relate the judgments God would take on David's enemies. He concluded by writing that he was poor and sorrowful but that he knew God's salvation would set him in a high place (v. 29).

When you find yourself like David, grab on to the promises of this psalm. Despite your circumstances you, too, can praise the name of God with a song and can magnify Him with thanksgiving while you are expecting His gracious answer to your plight.

Prayer

Dear heavenly Father, I pray You will give me a burden for souls. Help me pray faithfully for my children and grandchildren who are not living for You. If they are not saved, please save them before they die. Make the reality of hell very clear to me so I may be a faithful witness to all of my loved ones when I present the gospel to them. In Christ's name I ask this, amen.

— —

Day 28
David's Mighty Men ... Except for Joab

Daily Bible Reading: 2 Samuel 23 and Psalm 68

Today's Verse: "These be the names of the mighty men whom David had." (2 Samuel 23:8)

Bible Lesson: This chapter begins with the declaration: "Now these be the last words of David." This was David's last written account of his life before he died.

David declared himself as "the son of Jesse, the man who was raised up on high, the anointed of the God of Jacob, the sweet psalmist of Israel" (v. 1). God blessed him with both musical and prophetic abilities. David continued, remembering God's blessings and mercies to him in raising him from a lowly shepherd to king of God's people Israel, and in making an eternal covenant with both him and his posterity. David reminded the readers about God's protection while they followed Him and also warned them about the destruction of the wicked.

David started to make a list of his mighty men (v. 8). He knew his success in wars (he never lost a battle) was due not only to his expertise and might but also to his mighty men, whom he had the privilege of commanding. He continued to list by name thirty-seven of his most worthy men and some of their notable exploits.

As you read this list carefully, noting those worthy men who fought alongside David to help make him successful, you will notice there is one name missing. That name is Joab.

David's nephew Joab was captain of the host; he was a great military leader. He was with David in just about every battle and was an excellent warrior. Yet he is only referred to in this list as a qualifier.

The names of his two brothers appear here, as does his armor bearer, but Joab, himself, is not named.

No doubt, David thought of Joab as he penned these words and thought about his mighty men. Perhaps Joab was on his mind with the reference to "the sons of Belial" (v. 6). Joab, despite his noble service for King David, murdered three people who were special to David: Abner, Absalom, and Amasa. Joab knew David's desire toward all three of these men was life, not death, but in total self-will he rebelled against the commands of his king. Not only did Joab eventually pay for these deaths with his own life, but despite his military achievements, he is not mentioned in this chapter of David's hall of heroes.

Ponderings of a Woman after God's Heart: Hebrews 13:17 reads, "Obey them that have the rule over you, and submit yourselves: for they watch for your souls, as they that must give account, that they may do it with joy, and not with grief: for that is unprofitable for you." Joab did not obey and did not submit to him who had the rule over him. His self-will eventually became unprofitable for him.

This verse is in reference to those God places in church leadership because they "watch for your souls." Your pastor will give account to God concerning you, but it is up to you and your actions as to what he will say to God about you. If your pastor gives a bad report to God about you, there is the solemn warning that this will be unprofitable for you. Take a few moments now to assess your relationship with your church and to consider what your pastor may say to God about you.

Giving an account to God for you is a very serious responsibility for your pastor. Being part of a local church puts you under church leadership, which is God's will for every Christian. I wonder about those Christians who do not attend church and therefore do not have anyone who watches for their souls. Who will give an account to God for them?

Thoughts on Psalm 138: David possibly penned this encouraging psalm as an older king, looking back over all of the wonderful works of God toward him throughout the years.

Verse three is particularly comforting. David wrote, "In the day when I cried thou answeredst me, and strengthenedst me with strength in my soul." When you pray and you don't receive the answer you desire right away, don't think God has not heard you. Rather, this verse tells us God will strengthen your soul while you wait for His answer. So no matter what God's answer may be—a quick yes, a no, or your least favorite, wait—know that when you cry out to your heavenly Father, He really does hear. Thank Him and go in His strength as you wait for His answer.

David realized he still might have trouble (v. 7). God does not take trials away from His children, yet David understood that through his troubles, God would be with him to both revive and perfect him. Whatever you may be facing as you read this, I encourage you to praise God for His goodness and for His daily strength to you. God truly is good.

Prayer

Dear heavenly Father, thank You for my church, my pastor, and all of the other spiritual leaders who watch for my soul. Help me to work with them so that when they do give an account to God for me, it will truly be with joy. Help them to serve You well in the local church. In Christ's name I ask this. Amen.

- -

Day 29
David Numbers the People

Daily Bible Reading: 1 Chronicles 21 and Psalm 150

Today's Verse: "At that time when David saw that the Lord had answered him in the threshing floor of Ornan the Jebusite, then he sacrificed there." (1 Chronicles 21:28)

Bible Lesson: David was nearing the end of his life in this portion of Scripture. Satan tempted him to find out the military strength of his nation (v. 1). Why? This could have been a source of pride for the aging king, and Satan knew it was a weak spot he could exploit. Prior to this, David trusted in God, no matter if he had many people or few.

Joab immediately recognized the folly of this census-taking order from the king. He faithfully protested, telling King David that no matter how many people there were, they were all the king's servants, and this action was unnecessary. Nevertheless, the king's word was law, so Joab did as he was ordered, but he purposely omitted two tribes (v. 6).

God was displeased. He sent the prophet Gad to David, telling him there would be consequences for this foolish action. And then on orders from God, Gad came to David (v. 10) with one of three choices of punishment:

Three years of famine over all of Israel.

Three months of being destroyed by their enemies.

Three days of God destroying some of the people.

In each of these choices, some of the population (which had just been numbered) would be significantly reduced. David replied that he wanted to fall into the "hand of the Lord; for very great are His mercies" (v. 13). So God sent pestilence upon the children of Israel, which continued for three days and killed seventy thousand men. During this epidemic, David and the elders of Israel prayed and fasted while clothed in sackcloth—a rough type of material worn as a garment that symbolized humility and repentance toward God. God heard David's prayers and gave a message to Gad, instructing David to erect an altar to the Lord in a particular place—Ornan's threshing floor.

Ornan was threshing wheat with his four sons when they saw the destroying angel. Next, Ornan saw the royal procession with King David in the lead. David then requested Ornan's threshing floor to build an altar so the deadly plague would stop.

Ornan, quite unlike Nabal in David's younger days, was only too happy to oblige his king. He offered not only his threshing floor but also his oxen, his wooden instruments, and his wheat. He said, "I give it all" (v. 23). David countered, saying he would not take anything for the Lord at no cost. He paid Ornan, built the altar, and sacrificed to the Lord. This became the site where David later commanded Solomon to build the future temple (2 Chronicles 3:1).

Ponderings of a Woman after God's Heart: David set the example of sacrificial giving in this chapter. When Ornan offered his threshing floor to the king freely and without cost, David declined. David needed to make a personal sacrifice to God, and making a sacrifice costs.

Money is a very powerful possession. We like to gather it, but sometimes we are very careful in doling it out, perhaps too careful, even in the work of the Lord. Serving God is not without cost. We give to God with our time, and time can be money. Taking time out of our moneymaking activities to attend church is a sacrifice. Giving our hard-earned money to our local church takes money from our bank account. Giving our money is a type of service to Him.

It is God who gives us the ability to earn money. While ten percent of our money, the tithe, belongs to God through our local church, giving above and beyond that is sacrificial giving. Loving God and giving your money to Him is not a waste. Rather, it is an investment in heavenly and eternal rewards (Matthew 6:20).

Thoughts on Psalm 150: Psalm 150 is the last chapter in the book of Psalms. This gloriously happy and joyful song of praise to God is believed to be penned by David. The psalm reminds all of God's children to praise Him, for He is worthy of praise. He has created us, He has saved us from hell, He has brought us into His family, and we are part of His bride. He has done and is doing so many wonderful things for us, and He desires and deserves all of our heartfelt praise.

The mighty God, the Creator, the One who literally owns everything, wants to hear praise from all of His creation. Verse 6 commands, "Let every thing that hath breath praise the Lord." Praise is a gift we can and should give to our heavenly Father because He is our great Creator.

In your prayer time today, make sure you spend some time praising God for His mighty acts and for His excellent greatness in your personal life. You will run out of time before you exhaust all of the wonderful things you have to praise God for! I encourage you today and every day of your life to make praising God a habit. Praise is truly the gift you can give to the One who has given everything.

Prayer

Dear heavenly Father, please make me a cheerful giver. Help me to understand that You will not be indebted to anyone. Help me to give of my money, my time, and my talent cheerfully for Your service, knowing I am making an eternal investment. You are the source of all my income, and you have promised to meet all my needs. Help me to be grateful to You for all You have given me, and to give back to You in a great way. In the name of Jesus I ask this, amen.

— —

Day 30
David's Inheritance to Solomon

Daily Bible Reading: 1 Chronicles 22; Psalm 86

Today's Verse: "In my trouble I have prepared for the house of the Lord a hundred thousand talents of gold, and a thousand talents of silver; and of brass and iron without weight; for it is in abundance: timber also and stone have I prepared; and thou mayest add thereto." (1 Chronicles 22:14)

Bible Lesson: David chose the threshing floor of Ornan as the site of the future temple. We read that David's overwhelming desire, from the time he became king until he died, was to build the house of God. David had presented God with his desire, but God told him no (2 Samuel 7), that it would not be David—since he made war and shed much blood—but his son, a man of peace, who would build Him a house. David was now an old man, and his son Solomon would be the next king. Some Bible scholars believe Solomon was about eighteen years old at this time. David wanted to leave an inheritance for his son, and this inheritance was not money; it was all Solomon would need to build the house of God.

In this chapter, we see David organizing and gathering all of the raw materials for this magnificent house of worship. Some of the materials were iron for nails, brass, and cedar trees from afar in great abundance. Money was no object. It almost seemed as if David wanted to invest the entire treasury of his nation to build this house of worship for his God.

Not only did David work to provide the materials, he also counseled Solomon in depth as to exactly what to do in order to complete the temple. He explained to Solomon the temple was his idea but that because of his many wars, God denied him his request. He reminded Solomon that God promised David's dynasty would continue forever, and he further instructed Solomon to seek the Lord and to keep His law because the Lord would give him the wisdom he would need. David then commanded the princes of Israel, possibly Solomon's half-brothers, to help the new king in this task.

Ponderings of a Woman after God's Heart: David's son Solomon said "A good man leaves an inheritance to his children's children" (Proverbs 13:22). As a woman, I hope you, too, desire to leave an inheritance to your children. You may or may not be saving money for your children, or perhaps even for your grandchildren. Maybe you are reading this book and can barely make financial ends meet for yourself. Let me encourage you that an inheritance is not necessarily composed of money or other physical blessings. Starting today, no matter what your financial status may be, you can and should strive to leave your children and your grandchildren a spiritual inheritance. This type of inheritance will not only touch their physical lives but will last into eternity.

Suppose you don't have any children. Invest the truths of God's Word into the hearts and lives of those who are young, whether or not they are your biological offspring. It is up to us who are older to make sure those who are younger know the truths of God's Word. Part of our duty toward God is to pass on His Word.

The money you give to your church is part of your spiritual inheritance. Other ways to invest in a spiritual inheritance to future generations are: spending time in prayer, wise counsel, setting an example of godly living, and encouraging those who serve in your church. Touching lives to encourage godly living is a serious responsibility. Understand that leaving a spiritual inheritance to the next generation not only makes all the difference in the world but in heaven too.

Thoughts on Psalm 72: David wrote his last psalm as a blessing for his son Solomon. Having established Solomon on the throne, David left Solomon, his psalm-writing career, and soon, his mortal life also, with this prayer to God for His blessing on the new king.

David prayed Solomon's reign would be both peaceful and prosperous. Solomon would be great because he would have compassion on the poor and the needy and he would be just, not sparing the wicked who murder the innocent (v. 7).

David closed his last psalm with praise to the Lord, the God of Israel (v. 18). He continued his praise to God in verse 19, writing, "Blessed be his glorious name for ever: and let the whole earth be filled with his glory; Amen, and Amen." David was looking far beyond Solomon's reign with the desire that the whole earth would be filled with the glory of Christ's coming kingdom.

Prayer

Dear heavenly Father, help me to realize just how important a spiritual inheritance is now. Help me to invest in myself to be more God-fearing and God-honoring in all I do, knowing my actions will affect future generations. Help me to live for You, not only for myself but for a far greater influence because my inheritance is not only to my own children and grandchildren, but also to other young people. Help me to work today to leave behind a strong spiritual inheritance for them. I ask this in the name of the Savior, Christ Jesus, amen.

— —

Epilogue

David's Death and the Aftermath

Bible Reading: 1 Kings 2 and Psalm 127

Today's Verses: "David was thirty years old when he began to reign, and he reigned forty years." 1Kings 2:10–12 "David slept with his fathers, and was buried in the city of David. And the days that David reigned over Israel were forty years: seven years reigned he in Hebron, and thirty and three years reigned he in Jerusalem. Then sat Solomon upon the throne of David his father; and his kingdom was established greatly." (2 Samuel 5:4)

David died at age seventy after reigning as king over the nation of Israel for forty years. A record of the crown being passed from King David to his son Solomon is found in 1 Kings 2. Before David died he had words of wisdom and instructions to pass onto his son. He reminded Solomon to follow all of the commandments of God. Then he told him what to do concerning certain individuals who did him both good and evil, especially during the last few years of his reign.

After becoming king, and in obedience to David's wishes, Solomon had Joab executed. Furthermore, Solomon executed his half-brother Adonijah because Adonijah attempted to take the kingdom for himself. Adonijah was the fourth and last of David's sons who died as a result of his sin with Bathsheba. Mercifully, Adonijah died after David, so David was not alive to bear this additional grief. In the fourth year of Solomon's reign, he started to build the temple of the Lord and completed it seven years later.

Psalm 127 is a psalm of David, a song of degrees, which he wrote especially for Solomon. It is commonly believed songs of degrees were traveling songs sung by worshippers on their way to Jerusalem. This short, simple psalm is good advice from a father to his son concerning business and family life.

Dear Friend

Dear friend, thank you for reading my book. It is a great honor to me that you have chosen to read what I have written. But before you go, I want to ask you a very personal question: Are you absolutely sure that when you die you are bound for heaven?

Many women call themselves "Christian" because they believe in God, Jesus, and even the Holy Spirit, and this is all very good. They may pray to Jesus too. But Jesus Himself addressed this when He said,

> Not every one that saith unto me, Lord, Lord, shall enter into the kingdom of heaven; but he that doeth the will of my Father which is in heaven. Many will say to me in that day, Lord, Lord, have we not prophesied in thy name? and in thy name have cast out devils? and in thy name done many wonderful works? And then will I profess unto them, I never knew you: depart from me, ye that work iniquity.
>
> —Matthew 7:21–23

Wow! These are very powerful and harsh words! Jesus is saying He will personally tell some people to depart from Him, to actually go into hell, even though while they were alive they prophesied in His name, cast out devils, and did many wonderful works. What they did may be more than what you've ever done or will ever do.

My desire, and even more importantly God's desire, for you is that you know for sure that when you do meet Jesus face-to-face, He will welcome you into His holy heaven forever instead of saying, 'Depart from me, ye that work iniquity." If you have any doubts about this, I pray you would make sure of this now.

The Bible, God's Holy Word to mankind, records, "These things have I written unto you that believe on the name of the Son of God; that ye may know that ye have eternal life, and that ye may believe on the name of the Son of God" (1 John 5:13). You can know *now* that you are assured of Jesus welcoming you into heaven when you die. Jesus said, "Ye must be born again" (John 3:7). Since He has made being born again a requirement for both salvation and heaven, He also tells you how to become born again.

You must first realize that you are a sinner and that your sins have separated you from God. "All have sinned, and come short of the glory of God" (Romans 3:23). As a sinner, you are condemned to death. "The wages of sin is death" (Romans 6:23). We have all earned those wages! This death is not only physical death but even more seriously, spiritual death, which is eternal separation from God in hell. "It is appointed unto men once to die, but after this the judgement" (Hebrews 9:27). After you physically die, you will still be spiritually alive to be judged of God and to see if He deems you worthy to enter His heaven.

The certain news is that you cannot enter heaven as a sinful human being. The good news is that Jesus Himself took your punishment for sin and died on the cross in your place. "God commendeth [shows] His love toward us, in that, while we were yet sinners, Christ died for us" (Romans 5:8).

God also tells you to repent: "God ... commandeth all men everywhere to repent" (Acts 17:30). Repentance is a change of mind, which agrees with God that you are a sinner. Repentance also means you agree that Jesus died for your sins on the cross.

If you believe Jesus took your sins, died in your place, was buried, and then after three days and three nights rose from the dead, then you can truly call on the name of the Lord to be saved. Romans 10:14 promises us "whosoever shall call upon the name of the Lord shall be saved." God also recorded in His Holy Word that when the apostle Paul and his friend Silas were asked, "What must I do to be saved?" they replied, "Believe on the Lord Jesus Christ, and thou shalt be saved" (Acts 16:30–31).

If you have any doubts you are saved, or fear you would not be welcomed into heaven, you can pray right now to God, asking Him to save you. You can use this sample prayer:

Dear Jesus, I know I am a sinner. I believe, and I thank You for taking my sins on Yourself when You died on the cross. I believe You bled, died, and were buried, and three days later You were resurrected. All that You did so long ago was for me now. Please come into my heart and save me from hell. Thank You for Your forgiveness of my sins and Your gift of heaven and everlasting life.

If you prayed this prayer and sincerely and humbly meant it—you have called upon the name of the Lord Jesus Christ and believed on the Lord Jesus Christ—you are saved. You now have the assurance of going to heaven when you die. You made a very wise decision. The Bible tells us "that if thou shalt confess with thy mouth the Lord Jesus, and shalt believe in thine heart that God hath raised him from the dead, thou shalt be saved. For with the heart man believeth unto righteousness; and with the mouth confession is made unto salvation" (Romans 10:9–10).

This action cannot be undone. You are now a child of God, and His Holy Spirit is living within you. Do not be afraid to tell others about what you did. The same God Who saved you is ready and willing to save your family and friends so they, too, can be assured of heaven.

Sincerely,
Mary Jane Hames

\- \-

Glossary

Abiathar – A priest of the Lord, the son of Ahimelech the priest.

Abigail – David's second wife, widow of Nabal.

Abimelech – Title of Philistine kings meaning "father, king." Achish—the king of Gath—is also referred to as Abimelech.

Abinadab – David's older brother who served in Saul's army.

Abishai – Brother of Joab and Asahel, a nephew of David and chief of his mighty men.

Abner – Uncle of King Saul and chief commander of Saul's army. He was murdered by Joab.

Absalom – David's son who led a rebellion against him for the kingdom and was killed by Joab.

Achish – Philistine king of Gath who helped David twice when he was fleeing from Saul.

Adonijah – Son of David, half-brother to Solomon, who tried to claim the kingdom. He was executed by Solomon after David's death and was the fourth of David's sons to die.

Adullam – A cave where David and his men hid from Saul.

Ahimelech – A priest of the Lord under King Saul.

Ahithophel – David's counselor who deserted David to go with Absalom when Absalom tried to usurp the kingdom.

Amnon – David's firstborn son who was murdered by his half-brother Absalom.

Amasa – David's nephew through his sister Abigail. He was promoted to the position of captain of the host instead of Joab by Absalom, in his rebellion, but David retained him in this position to replace Joab. He was then murdered by Joab.

Asahel – Brother of Joab, nephew of David, one of David's mighty men.

Baanah – Brother of Rechab, captain of one of Saul's bands. He murdered Saul's son Ishbosheth with his brother Rechab. Both men were executed by David.

Bathsheba – Wife of Uriah, she was the object of David's adulterous affair and eventually one of David's wives. She was the mother of Solomon, the third king of Israel.

Benjamin – The smallest tribe of Israel. Saul was from this tribe.

City of David – Another name for Jerusalem.

Doeg the Edomite – One of Saul's men who told Saul David communicated with Ahimelech the priest.

Eliab – David's oldest brother who served in Saul's army.

Engedi – A wilderness where David first spared Saul's life.

Gath – One of the royal cities of the Philistines. The giant Goliath was from Gath, and David fled to Achish king of Gath when Saul was pursuing him.

God – Old Testament name of God from the Hebrew *Elohim*, which means, "the mighty One, the putter forth of power, the powerful One." This is plural in Hebrew, indicating the three-person Godhead.

Goliath – The giant David defeated with a stone and a sling.

Hiram, King of Tyre – A friend of both David and Solomon. He provided materials to David to build him a house in Jerusalem and also provided the building materials for the temple.

House of Judah – The members of the tribes of Judah and Benjamin.

Hushai the Archite – David's friend who served as an undercover agent for David when Absalom tried to take the kingdom. He defeated the counsel of Ahithophel.

Ishbosheth – Saul's son who was anointed king of Israel by Abner.

Ittai – A non-Israelite man who was loyal to King David during Absalom's revolt.

Jebusites – The original and idolatrous inhabitants of Jerusalem.

Jerusalem – The city David and his men captured and made the capital of Israel.

Jesse – David's father.

Joab – David's nephew who served as a captain in David's army.

Jonathan – David's best friend and brother-in-law, Saul's son.

Judah – Also known as the house of Judah, the southern part of Israel comprising the tribes of Judah and Benjamin. Its capital was Jerusalem.

Keilah – A city on the lowlands of Judah.

Keilah – A city the Philistines fought against. David and his men saved the city, but the men of Israel were going to deliver David into Saul's hand.

Lodebar – A town where Mephibosheth lived before David found him.

Lord – Old Testament name of God from the Hebrew *Adonai* meaning "master."

Lord – One of the three Old Testament names of God, spelled in all capital letters. It's from the Hebrew *Jehovah,* the personal name of God. This name implies a personal relationship/friendship with God.

Maon – A wilderness where David hid from Saul, the area where David met Abigail.

Mephibosheth – A son of Jonathan who was lame on both of his feet. David showed kindness to him.

Merah – Saul's oldest daughter, originally arranged to marry David.

Michal – Saul's younger daughter who loved David and became his first wife.

Nabal – Abigail's first husband. His name means "fool."

Naioth – A college for prophets most likely established by Samuel near Ramah.

Nathan – A prophet of God during most of David's reign.

Nob – A city of priests.

Obed-edom – A man whose house held the ark of God for three months.

Ornan – Owner of the threshing floor David bought to sacrifice to the Lord in to stop the deadly plague. This site became the area of the future temple of Solomon.

Phaltiel – Michal's second husband, who followed her weeping when her brother Ishbosheth took her from him to give her back to David.

Philistines – The ancient enemies of Israel.

Rabbah – The royal city of the Ammonites Joab conquered while David remained in Jerusalem.

Rechab – A brother of Baanah, captain of one of Saul's bands who helped Baanah murder Saul's son Ishbosheth. Both men were executed by David.

Samuel – A prophet of God who anointed David king of Israel.

Saul – The first king of Israel.

Selah – This word is found in the book of Psalms and three times in Habakkuk 3. It is actually a musical notation, a rest. It is provided for the reader to stop reading and to meditate on the passage of Scripture.

Shammah – David's older brother who served in Saul's army.

Sons of Belial – A name for people who were evil. Belial is another name for the devil.

Sons of Kohath – Particular priests of the tribe of Levi who were to carry the vessels of the tabernacle on their shoulders (Numbers 7:9).

Uzzah – A man who touched the ark of God to steady it when the cart's oxen stumbled. God killed him for this act.

Zeruiah – David's sister, mother of Abishai, Joab, and Asahel.

Ziklag – A city in Gath that was given to David before he became king of Israel.

Zion – Another name for Jerusalem. It means "monument."

Ziph – The name of the wilderness area where David spared Saul's life the second time.

Acknowledgments

All glory to David's God who is my God also. Thank You for giving Your holy living Word that is "profitable for doctrine, for reproof, for correction, for instruction in righteousness" (2 Timothy 3:16). The life of David is no exception. Despite his sins and his failures, he never stopped loving You. He never worshiped and served any other gods. May we learn from his example. Thank You for helping me with writing this book.

Special thanks to my wonderful Sunday school students: Verna, Emily, Josiah, and Destiny, who learned about the life of David with me.

To my husband, Joseph, who took my convoluted sentences and made them easy to read without changing what I wanted to express, while all the time encouraging me. I do thank you so very much for your help; I could not have done this without you.

To Pastor Kevin Kline of Victory Bible Church in Paxinos, Pennsylvania, who asked me to teach Sunday school. That action started my thoughts that eventually led to this book. Thank you also for teaching me how to think about the Bible.

To Mrs. Kay Kline of Paxinos, Pennsylvania, who graciously proofed my work, putting in necessary commas and missing words to make my words flow.

To my uncle, Ralph Hornberger of Trevose, Pennsylvania, who thoroughly and meticulously polished every word. He helped me get everything in the right tense, showed me where to use semicolons, and caught important points I overlooked. God sent him as an answer to my prayer for an editor. Uncle Ralph, you made my work so much more special by not only your excellent and through grammatical input conveyed by your faithful red (and black) pens, but because it was my very own, favorite uncle who contributed to my efforts. Thank you so much. You are the best!

About the Author

Photo by Lindsey Hoke

Mary Jane Humes's desire to learn, coupled with a bit of adventure, led her into several various job positions, a few of which actually utilized her BA in biology. Raised on a steady diet of books but no TV, she always had a dream of writing a book someday, so she did. *David's Faith* is her first book. Currently she teaches Sunday school and plays the piano for her church.

When Mary Jane is not writing, she loves working on her property with her husband, Joseph, and caring for all of their rescued furry little ones.

Contact
LinkedIn: www.linkedin.com/in/mary-jane-humes
Facebook: www.facebook.com/mjhumes
Email: hello@maryjanehumes.com
Website: maryjanehumes.com

Can You Help?

Reviews are everything to an author, because they mean a book is given more visibility. If you enjoyed this book, please review it on your favorite book review sites and tell your friends about it. Thank you!

Don't miss out!

Visit the website below and you can sign up to receive emails whenever Mary Jane Humes publishes a new book. There's no charge and no obligation.

https://books2read.com/r/B-A-RTCP-NGSPB

BOOKS 2 READ

Connecting independent readers to independent writers.

Also by Mary Jane Humes

Faith Series Devotionals
Naaman's Faith
David's Faith: A 30 Day Women's Devotional Based on the Life of King David
Esther's Faith - A 30-Day Bible Study Devotional for Women Based on the Book of Esther
Joseph's Faith: A 30-Day Bible Study Devotional for Women Based on the Life of Joseph from the Book of Genesis
Abraham's Faith A 30-Day Bible Study Devotional for Women Based on the Life of Abraham

Watch for more at https://www.maryjanehumes.com.

About the Author

Mary Jane Humes is a Bible teacher who always wanted to write a book. When she realized that many adults did not know the Bible stories that she was teaching in her Sunday school class, nor did they realzie the spiritual value of have a daily time of Bible reading and prayer, she decided to write a series of Bible study devotionals. Although her books are slanted toward women, men like reading them too. Currently she is finishing writing her fourth devotional - Sarah's Faith.

When she is not writing - which she found is a good excuse to avoid housework - she enjoys working outside with her husband Joe at their home in Pennsylvania.

Read more at https://www.maryjanehumes.com.

www.ingramcontent.com/pod-product-compliance
Lightning Source LLC
LaVergne TN
LVHW011425080426
835512LV00005B/267